Cram101 Textbook Outlines to accompany:

Taking Sides: Clashing Views on Controversial Legal Issues

Katsh & Rose, 11th Edition

An Academic Internet Publishers (AIPI) publication (c) 2007.

Cram101 and Cram101.com are AIPI publications and services. All notes, highlights, reviews, and practice tests are prepared by AIPI for use in AIPI publications, all rights reserved.

You have a discounted membership at www.Cram101.com with this book.

Get all of the practice tests for the chapters of this textbook, and access in-depth reference material for writing essays and papers. Here is an example from a Cram101 Biology text:

When you need problem solving help with math, stats, and other disciplines, www.Cram101.com will walk through the formulas and solutions step by step.

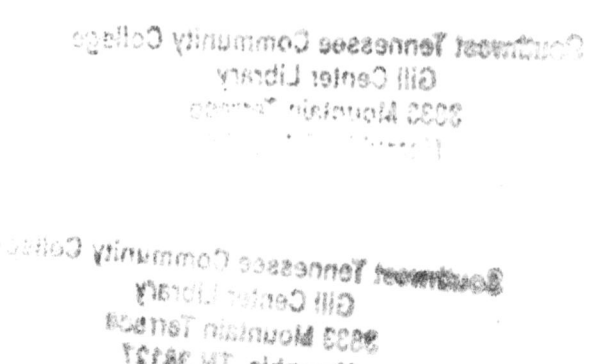

With Cram101.com online, you also have access to extensive reference material.

You will nail those essays and papers. Here is an example from a Cram101 Biology text:

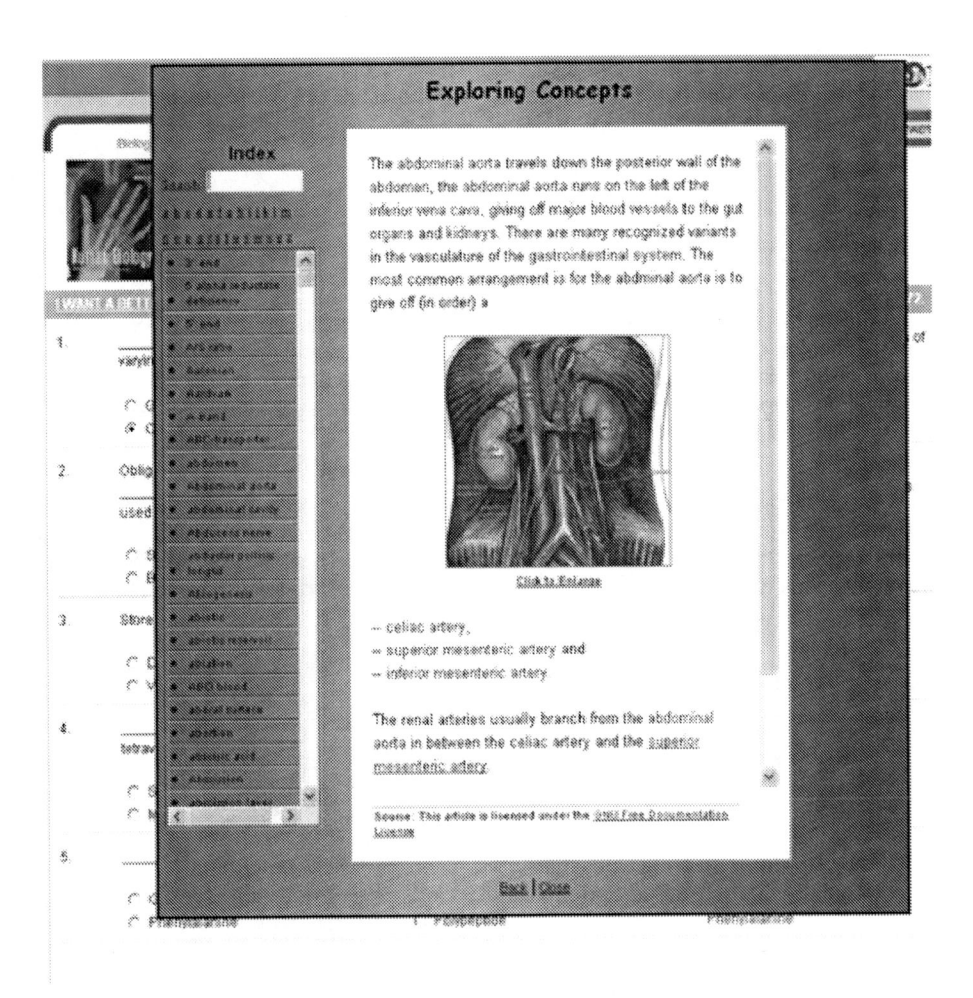

Visit **www.Cram101.com**, click Sign Up at the top of the screen, and enter DK73DW2431 in the promo code box on the registration screen. Access to www.Cram101.com is normally $9.95, but because you have purchased this book, your access fee is only $4.95. Sign up and stop highlighting textbooks forever.

Learning System

Cram101 Textbook Outlines is a learning system. The notes in this book are the highlights of your textbook, you will never have to highlight a book again.

How to use this book. Take this book to class, it is your notebook for the lecture. The notes and highlights on the left hand side of the pages follow the outline and order of the textbook. All you have to do is follow along while your intructor presents the lecture. Circle the items emphasized in class and add other important information on the right side. With Cram101 Textbook Outlines you'll spend less time writing and more time listening. Learning becomes more efficient.

Cram101.com Online

Increase your studying efficiency by using Cram101.com's practice tests and online reference material. It is the perfect complement to Cram101 Textbook Outlines. Use self-teaching matching tests or simulate in-class testing with comprehensive multiple choice tests, or simply use Cram's true and false tests for quick review. Cram101.com even allows you to enter your in-class notes for an integrated studying format combining the textbook notes with your class notes.

Visit **www.Cram101.com**, click Sign Up at the top of the screen, and enter **DK73DW2431** in the promo code box on the registration screen. Access to www.Cram101.com is normally $9.95, but because you have purchased this book, your access fee is only $4.95. Sign up and stop highlighting textbooks forever.

Copyright © 2008 by Academic Internet Publishers, Inc. All rights reserved. "Cram101"® and "Never Highlight a Book Again!"® are registered trademarks of Academic Internet Publishers, Inc. The Cram101 Textbook Outline series is printed in the United States. ISBN(s): 1-4288-2436-7 perfect-bound, and 1-4288-2437-5 spiral bound.

Taking Sides: Clashing Views on Controversial Legal Issues
Katsh & Rose, 11th

CONTENTS

1. Standardless Manual Recounts 2
2. Is Abortion Protected by the Constitution? 6
3. Are Restrictions on Physician-Assisted Suicide Constitutional? 12
4. Do People Have a Legal Right to Clone Themselves? 18
5. Does the Sharing of Music Files Through the Internet Violate Copyright Laws? 20
6. Should the Insanity Defense Be Abolished? 24
7. Are Pretextual Stops by the Police Constitutional? 28
8. Do Religious Groups Have a Right to Use Public School Facilities After Hours? 32
9. Fourth Amendment Search and Seizure Guarantee 36
10. Laws Requiring Schools and Libraries to Filter Internet Access 40
11. Is It Constitutional to Impose the Death Penalty on the Mentally Retarded? 46
12. Is a Sentence of Life in Prison for Stealing $150 Constitutional? 50
13. Drug Use Testing of Students Who Participate in Extracurricular Activities 54
14. Can Companies That Lie About Their Business Practices 58
15. Are Blanket Prohibitions on Cross Burnings Unconstitutional? 64
16. Are Laws Criminalizing Homosexual Conduct Unconstitutional? 70
17. Damages in Cases of Student-on-Student Sexual Harassment? 76
18. Extraordinary Care to Attend Regular Classes in Public Schools 80
19. Race-Conscious Programs in Public University Admissions Policies 82

Chapter 1. Standardless Manual Recounts

Due process	In United States law, adopted from English Law, due process is the principle that the government must normally respect all of a person's legal rights instead of just some or most of those legal rights when the government deprives a person of life, liberty, or property. Due process has also been frequently interpreted as placing limitations on laws and legal proceedings, in order for judges instead of legislators to guarantee fundamental fairness, justice, and liberty.
Constitution	A constitution is a system that establishes the rules and principles that govern an organization or political entity.
Supreme Court	The supreme court functions as a court of last resort whose rulings cannot be challenged, in some countries, provinces and states. However, in some jurisdictions other phrases are used to describe the highest courts. There are also some jurisdictions where the supreme court is not the highest court.
Dissenting opinion	A dissenting opinion is an opinion of one or more judges expressing disagreement with the majority opinion. A dissenting opinion cannot create binding precedent because the holding in the opinion is not the holding of the court in the case.
Democracy	Democracy is a form of government in which supreme power is vested in the people and exercised by them directly or indirectly through a system of representation usually involving periodic free elections.
Mandate	In international law, a mandate is a binding obligation issued from an inter-governmental organization like the United Nations to a country which is bound to follow the instructions of the organization.
Certiorari	Certiorari is a legal term in Roman, English and American law referring to a type of writ seeking judicial review. It is the present passive infinitive of Latin certioro, a contraction of certiorem facere.
Writ	In law, a writ is a formal written order issued by a body with administrative or judicial jurisdiction. In modern usage, this public body is normally a court. Warrants, prerogative writs, and subpoenas are types of writs, but there are many others.
Jurisdiction	In law, jurisdiction is the practical authority granted to a formally constituted legal body or to a political leader to deal with and make pronouncements on legal matters and, by implication, to administer justice within a defined area of responsibility.
Equal protection clause	The Equal Protection Clause, part of the Fourteenth Amendment to the United States Constitution, provides that "no state shall deny to any person within its jurisdiction the equal protection of the laws." The Equal Protection Clause can be seen as an attempt to secure the promise of the United States' professed commitment to the proposition that "all men are created equal" by empowering the judiciary to enforce that principle against the states.
Legislature	A legislature is a type of representative deliberative assembly with the power to adopt laws. In presidential systems of government, the legislature is considered a power branch which is equal to, and independent of, the executive.
Electoral college	An electoral college is a set of electors, who are empowered as a deliberative body to elect a candidate to a particular office. Often these electors represent a different organization or entity with each organization or entity represented by a particular number of electors or with votes weighted in a particular way.
Electorate	In politics, an electorate is the group of people entitled to vote in an election. The term can refer to:the totality of voters or electors the partisans of a particular individual, group or political party the collection of the voters enrolled in a geographically-defined area less commonly, the geographically-defined area which returns a representative.
Suffrage	Suffrage is the civil right to vote, or the exercise of that right. Universal suffrage is the term used to describe a situation in which the right to vote is not restricted by race, sex, belief or social status.
Case law	Case law the body of judge-made law and legal decisions that interprets prior case law, statutes and

Go to **Cram101.com** for the Practice Tests for this Chapter.

Chapter 1. Standardless Manual Recounts

Chapter 1. Standardless Manual Recounts

	other legal authority -- including doctrinal writings by legal scholars such as the Corpus Juris Secundum, Halsbury's Laws of England or the doctrinal writings found in the Recueil Dalloz and law commissions such as the American Law Institute.
Representative government	Representative government is a form of government founded on the principles of popular sovereignty by the people's representatives. The representatives are charged with the responsibility of acting in the people's interest, but not as their proxy representative.
Judicial review	Judicial review is the power of a court to review a law or an official act of a government employee or agent for constitutionality or for the violation of basic principles of justice. If a court has a power of judicial review, then the court has power to strike down that law, overturn that official act, or order a public official to act in a certain manner, if the court believes the law or act to be unconstitutional, or believes the law or act to be contrary to law in a free and democratic society.
Appellate jurisdiction	Appellate jurisdiction is the power of a court to review the decisions and change the outcomes of the decisions of previous, lower-level courts. The review process begins when a party or parties dissatisfied with the decision of the lower court appeal the decision to an appellate court. Depending on the court and the type of case, appellate review may consist of an entirely new hearing on the matter (a trial de novo), or may be limited to a review of particular legal rulings made by the inferior tribunal.
Judiciary	In the law, the judiciary is the system of courts which administer justice in the name of the sovereign or state, a mechanism for the resolution of disputes. The term is also used to refer collectively to the judges, magistrates and other adjudicators who form the core of a judiciary, as well as the support personnel who keep the system running smoothly.
Magistrate	A magistrate is a judicial officer. In common law systems a magistrate usually has limited authority to administer and enforce the law. In civil law systems a magistrate may be a judge of a superior court.
Delegate	A delegate is an individual or a member of a group called at the interests of a larger organization at a meeting of some kind. In order to avoid the principal-agent problem, it is generally important to the organization to take steps to ensure that the delegate does not have a conflict of interest.
Federal question	Federal question jurisdiction is a term used in the United States law of civil procedure to refer to the situation in which a United States federal court has subject matter jurisdiction to hear a civil case because the plaintiff has alleged a violation of the Constitution, laws, or treaties of the United States.
Rule of law	The rule of law is the principle that governmental authority is legitimately exercised only in accordance with written, publicly disclosed laws adopted and enforced in accordance with established procedure.
Partisan	In politics, partisan usually refers to a fervent, sometimes militant supporter or proponent of a party, cause, faction, person, or idea.
Legitimacy	Legitimacy in political science, is the popular acceptance of a governing regime or law as an authority. Where as authority refers to a specific position in an established government, the term legitimacy is used when describing a system of government itself —where "government may be generalized to mean the wider "sphere of influence."

Chapter 1. Standardless Manual Recounts

Chapter 2. Is Abortion Protected by the Constitution?

Constitution	A constitution is a system that establishes the rules and principles that govern an organization or political entity.
Majority opinion	In law, a majority opinion is a judicial opinion agreed to by a majority of the members of a court. A majority opinion sets forth the decision of the court and an explanation of the rationale behind the court's decision.
Supreme Court	The supreme court functions as a court of last resort whose rulings cannot be challenged, in some countries, provinces and states. However, in some jurisdictions other phrases are used to describe the highest courts. There are also some jurisdictions where the supreme court is not the highest court.
Dissenting opinion	A dissenting opinion is an opinion of one or more judges expressing disagreement with the majority opinion. A dissenting opinion cannot create binding precedent because the holding in the opinion is not the holding of the court in the case.
Due process	In United States law, adopted from English Law, due process is the principle that the government must normally respect all of a person's legal rights instead of just some or most of those legal rights when the government deprives a person of life, liberty, or property. Due process has also been frequently interpreted as placing limitations on laws and legal proceedings, in order for judges instead of legislators to guarantee fundamental fairness, justice, and liberty.
Medicaid	Medicaid is the US health insurance program for individuals and families with low incomes and resources. It is jointly funded by the states and federal government, and is managed by the states. Among the groups of people served by Medicaid are eligible low-income parents, children, seniors, and people with disabilities. Medicaid is the largest source of funding for medical and health-related services for people with limited income.
Case law	Case law the body of judge-made law and legal decisions that interprets prior case law, statutes and other legal authority -- including doctrinal writings by legal scholars such as the Corpus Juris Secundum, Halsbury's Laws of England or the doctrinal writings found in the Recueil Dalloz and law commissions such as the American Law Institute.
Amicus curiae	Amicus curiae, is a legal Latin phrase, literally translated as "friend of the court", that refers to someone, not a party to a case, who volunteers to offer information on a point of law or some other aspect of the case to assist the court in deciding a matter before it. The information may be a legal opinion in the form of a brief - testimony that has not been solicited by any of the parties - or a learned treatise on a matter that bears on the case. The decision whether to admit the information lies with the discretion of the court.
Injunction	An injunction is an equitable remedy in the form of a court order, whereby a party is required to do, or to refrain from doing, certain acts. The party that fails to adhere to the injunction faces civil or criminal penalties and may have to pay damages or accept sanctions for failing to follow the court's order. In some cases, breaches of injunctions are considered serious criminal offences that merit arrest and possible prison sentences.
Bench trial	A bench trial in the U.S. is a trial before a judge in which the right to a jury trial has been waived by the necessary parties. In the case of a criminal trial, in most states the criminal defendant alone has the ability to waive the right to a jury. In a civil trial, one of the parties must request a jury trial otherwise a bench trial will result.
Court of Appeal	Court of Appeal is the title of a court which has the power to consider or hear an appeal. A court of appeal is also a superior court.
Stare decisis	Stare decisis (Latin: [sta¢°re de¢° ki¢°si¢°s], Anglicisation: [sta¢° i də sa s s], "to stand by things decided") is a Latin legal term, used in common law to express the notion that prior court decisions must be recognized as precedents, according to case law. More

Chapter 2. Is Abortion Protected by the Constitution?

Chapter 2. Is Abortion Protected by the Constitution?

	fully, the legal term is "stare decisis et non quieta movere" meaning "stand by decisions and do not move that which is quiet" (the phrase "quieta non movere" is itself a famous maxim akin to "let sleeping dogs lie").
Mandate	In international law, a mandate is a binding obligation issued from an inter-governmental organization like the United Nations to a country which is bound to follow the instructions of the organization.
Autonomy	Autonomy means freedom from external authority. In politics, autonomy refers to self-governance.
Doctrine	Doctrine is a body of axioms fundamental to the exercise of a nation's foreign policy. Hence, doctrine, in this sense, has come to suggest a broad consistency that holds true across a spectrum of acts and actions.
Pragmatism	**Pragmatism** is a philosophic school that originated with Charles Sanders Peirce and came to fruition in the early twentieth-century philosophies of William James and John Dewey.
Rule of law	The rule of law is the principle that governmental authority is legitimately exercised only in accordance with written, publicly disclosed laws adopted and enforced in accordance with established procedure.
Constitutional law	Constitutional law is the study of foundational or basic laws of nation states and other political organizations. Constitutions are the framework for government and may limit or define the authority and procedure of political bodies to execute new laws and regulations.
Republic	A republic is a form of government maintained by a state or country whose sovereignty is based on popular consent and whose governance is based on popular representation and control. Several definitions stress the importance of the rule of law as among the requirements for a republic.
Judiciary	In the law, the judiciary is the system of courts which administer justice in the name of the sovereign or state, a mechanism for the resolution of disputes. The term is also used to refer collectively to the judges, magistrates and other adjudicators who form the core of a judiciary, as well as the support personnel who keep the system running smoothly.
Legitimacy	Legitimacy in political science, is the popular acceptance of a governing regime or law as an authority. Where as authority refers to a specific position in an established government, the term legitimacy is used when describing a system of government itself —where "government may be generalized to mean the wider "sphere of influence."
Litigation	A lawsuit, also known as litigation, is a criminal or civil action brought before a court in which the party commencing the action, the plaintiff, seeks a legal remedy. Often, one or more defendants are required to answer the plaintiff's complaint.
Plurality	A plurality, relative majority or simple majority is the largest share of something, which may or may not be considered a majority, i.e. it is the largest group/category, but is not necessarily a majority (more than half). In the U.S., simple majority has another meaning. The plurality voting system, also known as "First past the post", elects the candidate who is the stated first choice of the plurality of voters.
Common law	In common law legal systems, judges have the authority and duty to decide what the law is when there is no other authoritative statement of the law. Once an appellate court has decided what the law is, that precedent tends to bind future decisions of the same appellate court, and binds all lower courts reviewed by that appellate court, when the facts of the case are similar, until there is another authoritative statement of the law.
Legislature	A legislature is a type of representative deliberative assembly with the power to adopt laws. In presidential systems of government, the legislature is considered a power branch which is

Go to **Cram101.com** for the Practice Tests for this Chapter.

Chapter 2. Is Abortion Protected by the Constitution?

Chapter 2. Is Abortion Protected by the Constitution?

	equal to, and independent of, the executive.
Legislation	Legislation is law which has been promulgated (or "enacted") by a legislature or other governing body. The term may refer to a single law, or the collective body of enacted law, while "statute" is also used to refer to a single law. Before an item of legislation becomes law it may be known as a bill, which is typically also known as "legislation" while it remains under active consideration.
Punitive damages	Punitive damages are damages not awarded in order to compensate the plaintiff, but in order to reform or deter the defendant and similar persons from pursuing a course of action such as that which damaged the plaintiff. Punitive damages are often awarded where compensatory damages are deemed an inadequate remedy.
First Amendment	The First Amendment to the United States Constitution is a part of the United States Bill of Rights. It prohibits the federal legislature from making laws that establish religion or prohibit free exercise of religion, laws that infringe the freedom of
Euthanasia	**Euthanasia** is the practice of terminating the life of a person or animal in a presumably painless or minimally painful way, usually by lethal injection. Laws around the world vary greatly with regard to euthanasia and are constantly subject to change as cultural values shift and better palliative care or treatments become available.

Chapter 2. Is Abortion Protected by the Constitution?

Chapter 3. Are Restrictions on Physician-Assisted Suicide Constitutional?

Majority opinion	In law, a majority opinion is a judicial opinion agreed to by a majority of the members of a court. A majority opinion sets forth the decision of the court and an explanation of the rationale behind the court's decision.
Supreme Court	The supreme court functions as a court of last resort whose rulings cannot be challenged, in some countries, provinces and states. However, in some jurisdictions other phrases are used to describe the highest courts. There are also some jurisdictions where the supreme court is not the highest court.
Court of Appeal	Court of Appeal is the title of a court which has the power to consider or hear an appeal. A court of appeal is also a superior court.
Due process	In United States law, adopted from English Law, due process is the principle that the government must normally respect all of a person's legal rights instead of just some or most of those legal rights when the government deprives a person of life, liberty, or property. Due process has also been frequently interpreted as placing limitations on laws and legal proceedings, in order for judges instead of legislators to guarantee fundamental fairness, justice, and liberty.
Constitution	A constitution is a system that establishes the rules and principles that govern an organization or political entity.
Trial court	A trial court is the court in which most civil or criminal cases begin. Not all cases are heard in a trial court; some cases may begin in inferior limited jurisdiction bodies such as the case of the jurisdiction of an administrative body that has been created by statute to make some kind of binding determination under the law and were simplified procedural practices may apply similar to arbitration.
Euthanasia	**Euthanasia** is the practice of terminating the life of a person or animal in a presumably painless or minimally painful way, usually by lethal injection. Laws around the world vary greatly with regard to euthanasia and are constantly subject to change as cultural values shift and better palliative care or treatments become available.
Legislature	A legislature is a type of representative deliberative assembly with the power to adopt laws. In presidential systems of government, the legislature is considered a power branch which is equal to, and independent of, the executive.
Attorney General	The Attorney General is the main legal adviser to the government, and in some jurisdictions may in addition have executive responsibility for law enforcement or responsibility for public prosecutions.
Jurisdiction	In law, jurisdiction is the practical authority granted to a formally constituted legal body or to a political leader to deal with and make pronouncements on legal matters and, by implication, to administer justice within a defined area of responsibility.
Common law	In common law legal systems, judges have the authority and duty to decide what the law is when there is no other authoritative statement of the law. Once an appellate court has decided what the law is, that precedent tends to bind future decisions of the same appellate court, and binds all lower courts reviewed by that appellate court, when the facts of the case are similar, until there is another authoritative statement of the law.
Criminal law	Criminal law is the body of statutory and common law that deals with crime and the legal punishment of criminal offenses. It is law prohibiting conduct that disrupts social order or challenge's the authority of the state, and consequently deals with matters of significant public concern. In contrast with civil law, actions are pursued by the state rather than private citizens.
Initiative	In political science, the initiative provides a means by which a petition signed by a certain minimum number of registered voters can force a public vote on a proposed statute,

Chapter 3. Are Restrictions on Physician-Assisted Suicide Constitutional?

Chapter 3. Are Restrictions on Physician-Assisted Suicide Constitutional?

	constitutional amendment, charter amendment or ordinance, or, in its minimal form, to simply oblige the executive or legislative bodies to consider the subject by submitting it to the order of the day.
Bill of Rights	A bill of rights is a list or summary of which is considered important and essential by a group of people. The purpose of these bills is to protect those rights against infringement by other people and the government.
Plurality	A plurality, relative majority or simple majority is the largest share of something, which may or may not be considered a majority, i.e. it is the largest group/category, but is not necessarily a majority (more than half). In the U.S., simple majority has another meaning. The plurality voting system, also known as "First past the post", elects the candidate who is the stated first choice of the plurality of voters.
Dissenting opinion	A dissenting opinion is an opinion of one or more judges expressing disagreement with the majority opinion. A dissenting opinion cannot create binding precedent because the holding in the opinion is not the holding of the court in the case.
Case law	Case law the body of judge-made law and legal decisions that interprets prior case law, statutes and other legal authority -- including doctrinal writings by legal scholars such as the Corpus Juris Secundum, Halsbury's Laws of England or the doctrinal writings found in the Recueil Dalloz and law commissions such as the American Law Institute.
Judicial review	Judicial review is the power of a court to review a law or an official act of a government employee or agent for constitutionality or for the violation of basic principles of justice. If a court has a power of judicial review, then the court has power to strike down that law, overturn that official act, or order a public official to act in a certain manner, if the court believes the law or act to be unconstitutional, or believes the law or act to be contrary to law in a free and democratic society.
State action	A state action is a term used in United States civil rights law to describe a person who is acting on behalf of a governmental body, and is therefore subject to regulation under the United States bill of rights including the First, Fifth and Fourteenth Amendments, which prohibit the federal and state governments from violating certain rights and freedoms.
Doctrine	Doctrine is a body of axioms fundamental to the exercise of a nation's foreign policy. Hence, doctrine, in this sense, has come to suggest a broad consistency that holds true across a spectrum of acts and actions.
Autonomy	Autonomy means freedom from external authority. In politics, autonomy refers to self-governance.
Equal protection clause	The Equal Protection Clause, part of the Fourteenth Amendment to the United States Constitution, provides that "no state shall deny to any person within its jurisdiction the equal protection of the laws." The Equal Protection Clause can be seen as an attempt to secure the promise of the United States' professed commitment to the proposition that "all men are created equal" by empowering the judiciary to enforce that principle against the states.
Referendum	A referendum is a direct vote in which an entire electorate is asked to either accept or reject a particular proposal. This may be the adoption of a new constitution, a constitutional amendment, a law, the recall of an elected official or simply a specific government policy. The referendum is a form of direct democracy.
Judiciary	In the law, the judiciary is the system of courts which administer justice in the name of the sovereign or state, a mechanism for the resolution of disputes. The term is also used to refer collectively to the judges, magistrates and other adjudicators who form the core of a judiciary, as well as the support personnel who keep the system running smoothly.

Go to **Cram101.com** for the Practice Tests for this Chapter.

Chapter 3. Are Restrictions on Physician-Assisted Suicide Constitutional?

Chapter 3. Are Restrictions on Physician-Assisted Suicide Constitutional?

Mandate | In international law, a mandate is a binding obligation issued from an inter-governmental organization like the United Nations to a country which is bound to follow the instructions of the organization.

Civil liberties | Civil liberties is the name given to freedoms that completely protect the individual from government. Civil liberties set limits for government so that it can not abuse its power and interfere with the lives of its citizens.

Chapter 3. Are Restrictions on Physician-Assisted Suicide Constitutional?

Chapter 4. Do People Have a Legal Right to Clone Themselves?

Constitution	A constitution is a system that establishes the rules and principles that govern an organization or political entity.
Supreme Court	The supreme court functions as a court of last resort whose rulings cannot be challenged, in some countries, provinces and states. However, in some jurisdictions other phrases are used to describe the highest courts. There are also some jurisdictions where the supreme court is not the highest court.
Autonomy	Autonomy means freedom from external authority. In politics, autonomy refers to self-governance.
Legislation	Legislation is law which has been promulgated (or "enacted") by a legislature or other governing body. The term may refer to a single law, or the collective body of enacted law, while "statute" is also used to refer to a single law. Before an item of legislation becomes law it may be known as a bill, which is typically also known as "legislation" while it remains under active consideration.
Due process	In United States law, adopted from English Law, due process is the principle that the government must normally respect all of a person's legal rights instead of just some or most of those legal rights when the government deprives a person of life, liberty, or property. Due process has also been frequently interpreted as placing limitations on laws and legal proceedings, in order for judges instead of legislators to guarantee fundamental fairness, justice, and liberty.
Court of Appeal	Court of Appeal is the title of a court which has the power to consider or hear an appeal. A court of appeal is also a superior court.
Judicial review	Judicial review is the power of a court to review a law or an official act of a government employee or agent for constitutionality or for the violation of basic principles of justice. If a court has a power of judicial review, then the court has power to strike down that law, overturn that official act, or order a public official to act in a certain manner, if the court believes the law or act to be unconstitutional, or believes the law or act to be contrary to law in a free and democratic society.
Democracy	Democracy is a form of government in which supreme power is vested in the people and exercised by them directly or indirectly through a system of representation usually involving periodic free elections.
Criminal law	Criminal law is the body of statutory and common law that deals with crime and the legal punishment of criminal offenses. It is law prohibiting conduct that disrupts social order or challenge's the authority of the state, and consequently deals with matters of significant public concern. In contrast with civil law, actions are pursued by the state rather than private citizens.

Chapter 4. Do People Have a Legal Right to Clone Themselves?

Chapter 5. Does the Sharing of Music Files Through the Internet Violate Copyright Laws?

Majority opinion	In law, a majority opinion is a judicial opinion agreed to by a majority of the members of a court. A majority opinion sets forth the decision of the court and an explanation of the rationale behind the court's decision.
Court of Appeal	Court of Appeal is the title of a court which has the power to consider or hear an appeal. A court of appeal is also a superior court.
Amicus curiae	Amicus curiae, is a legal Latin phrase, literally translated as "friend of the court", that refers to someone, not a party to a case, who volunteers to offer information on a point of law or some other aspect of the case to assist the court in deciding a matter before it. The information may be a legal opinion in the form of a brief - testimony that has not been solicited by any of the parties - or a learned treatise on a matter that bears on the case. The decision whether to admit the information lies with the discretion of the court.
Doctrine	Doctrine is a body of axioms fundamental to the exercise of a nation's foreign policy. Hence, doctrine, in this sense, has come to suggest a broad consistency that holds true across a spectrum of acts and actions.
Supreme Court	The supreme court functions as a court of last resort whose rulings cannot be challenged, in some countries, provinces and states. However, in some jurisdictions other phrases are used to describe the highest courts. There are also some jurisdictions where the supreme court is not the highest court.
First Amendment	The First Amendment to the United States Constitution is a part of the United States Bill of Rights. It prohibits the federal legislature from making laws that establish religion or prohibit free exercise of religion, laws that infringe the freedom of
Injunction	An injunction is an equitable remedy in the form of a court order, whereby a party is required to do, or to refrain from doing, certain acts. The party that fails to adhere to the injunction faces civil or criminal penalties and may have to pay damages or accept sanctions for failing to follow the court's order. In some cases, breaches of injunctions are considered serious criminal offences that merit arrest and possible prison sentences.
Jurisdiction	In law, jurisdiction is the practical authority granted to a formally constituted legal body or to a political leader to deal with and make pronouncements on legal matters and, by implication, to administer justice within a defined area of responsibility.
Republic	A republic is a form of government maintained by a state or country whose sovereignty is based on popular consent and whose governance is based on popular representation and control. Several definitions stress the importance of the rule of law as among the requirements for a republic.
Plaintiff	A plaintiff is the party who initiates a lawsuit before a court. By doing so, the plaintiff seeks a legal remedy, and if successful, the court will issue judgment in favor of the plaintiff and make the appropriate court order .
Mandate	In international law, a mandate is a binding obligation issued from an inter-governmental organization like the United Nations to a country which is bound to follow the instructions of the organization.
Prior restraint	Prior restraint is a legal term referring to a government's actions that prevent materials from being published. Censorship that requires a person to seek governmental permission in the form of a license or imprimatur before publishing anything constitutes prior restraint every time permission is denied.
Constitution	A constitution is a system that establishes the rules and principles that govern an organization or political entity.
Public interest	The public interest refers to the "common well-being" or "general welfare." The public

Chapter 5. Does the Sharing of Music Files Through the Internet Violate Copyright Laws?

Chapter 5. Does the Sharing of Music Files Through the Internet Violate Copyright Laws?

	interest is central to policy debates, politics, democracy and the nature of government itself. While nearly everyone claims that aiding the common well-being or general welfare is positive, there is little, if any, consensus on what exactly constitutes the public interest.
Public good	In economics, a public good is a good that is non-rivalrous. This means: consumption of the good by one individual does not reduce the amount of the good available for consumption by others. For example, if one individual eats a cake, there is no cake left for anyone else; but breathing air or drinking water from a stream does not significantly reduce the amount of air or water available to others.
Judiciary	In the law, the judiciary is the system of courts which administer justice in the name of the sovereign or state, a mechanism for the resolution of disputes. The term is also used to refer collectively to the judges, magistrates and other adjudicators who form the core of a judiciary, as well as the support personnel who keep the system running smoothly.
Litigation	A lawsuit, also known as litigation, is a criminal or civil action brought before a court in which the party commencing the action, the plaintiff, seeks a legal remedy. Often, one or more defendants are required to answer the plaintiff's complaint.

Go to **Cram101.com** for the Practice Tests for this Chapter.

Chapter 5. Does the Sharing of Music Files Through the Internet Violate Copyright Laws?

Chapter 6. Should the Insanity Defense Be Abolished?

Judiciary	In the law, the judiciary is the system of courts which administer justice in the name of the sovereign or state, a mechanism for the resolution of disputes. The term is also used to refer collectively to the judges, magistrates and other adjudicators who form the core of a judiciary, as well as the support personnel who keep the system running smoothly.
Prime minister	A prime minister is the most senior minister of a cabinet in the executive branch of government in a parliamentary system.
Court of Appeal	Court of Appeal is the title of a court which has the power to consider or hear an appeal. A court of appeal is also a superior court.
Human nature	Human nature is the fundamental nature and substance of humans, as well as the range of human behavior that is, believed to be invariant over long periods of time and across very different cultural contexts.
Deterrence	Deterrence theory is a military strategy developed after and used throughout the Cold War and current times. It is especially relevant with regard to the use of nuclear weapons, and figures prominently on current United States foreign policy regarding the development of nuclear technology in North Korea and Iran.
Conservativism	Conservativism is a relativistic term used to describe political philosophies that favor traditional values, where "tradition" refers to religious, cultural, or nationally defined beliefs and customs.
Law and order	In politics, law and order refers to a political platform which supports a strict criminal justice system, especially in relation to violent crime and property crime, through harsher criminal penalties. These penalties may include longer terms of imprisonment, mandatory sentencing, and in some countries, capital punishment.
Cadre	Cadre are the backbone of an organization, usually a political organization. The assumption of the cadre model is that this small core of ultra-committed people are capable of recreating the organization's structure and ideological direction even if the current organizational form has been destroyed and all other members have been killed or imprisoned.
Treason	In law, treason is the crime of disloyalty to one's nation. A person who betrays the nation of their citizenship and/or reneges on an oath of loyalty and in some way willfully cooperates with an enemy.
Plea bargain	A plea bargain is an agreement in a criminal case in which a prosecutor and a defendant arrange to settle the case against the defendant. The defendant agrees to plead guilty or no contest in exchange for some agreement from the prosecutor as to the punishment.
Supreme Court	The supreme court functions as a court of last resort whose rulings cannot be challenged, in some countries, provinces and states. However, in some jurisdictions other phrases are used to describe the highest courts. There are also some jurisdictions where the supreme court is not the highest court.
Criminal law	Criminal law is the body of statutory and common law that deals with crime and the legal punishment of criminal offenses. It is law prohibiting conduct that disrupts social order or challenge's the authority of the state, and consequently deals with matters of significant public concern. In contrast with civil law, actions are pursued by the state rather than private citizens.
Legitimacy	Legitimacy in political science, is the popular acceptance of a governing regime or law as an authority. Where as authority refers to a specific position in an established government, the term legitimacy is used when describing a system of government itself —where "government may be generalized to mean the wider "sphere of influence."
Doctrine	Doctrine is a body of axioms fundamental to the exercise of a nation's foreign policy.

Go to **Cram101.com** for the Practice Tests for this Chapter.

Chapter 6. Should the Insanity Defense Be Abolished?

Chapter 6. Should the Insanity Defense Be Abolished?

	Hence, doctrine, in this sense, has come to suggest a broad consistency that holds true across a spectrum of acts and actions.
Common law	In common law legal systems, judges have the authority and duty to decide what the law is when there is no other authoritative statement of the law. Once an appellate court has decided what the law is, that precedent tends to bind future decisions of the same appellate court, and binds all lower courts reviewed by that appellate court, when the facts of the case are similar, until there is another authoritative statement of the law.
Euthanasia	**Euthanasia** is the practice of terminating the life of a person or animal in a presumably painless or minimally painful way, usually by lethal injection. Laws around the world vary greatly with regard to euthanasia and are constantly subject to change as cultural values shift and better palliative care or treatments become available.
Litigation	A lawsuit, also known as litigation, is a criminal or civil action brought before a court in which the party commencing the action, the plaintiff, seeks a legal remedy. Often, one or more defendants are required to answer the plaintiff's complaint.
Case law	Case law the body of judge-made law and legal decisions that interprets prior case law, statutes and other legal authority -- including doctrinal writings by legal scholars such as the Corpus Juris Secundum, Halsbury's Laws of England or the doctrinal writings found in the Recueil Dalloz and law commissions such as the American Law Institute.
Free Press	Free Press is a non-partisan, non-profit organization founded by media critic Robert McChesney to promote more democratic media policy in the United States.

Go to **Cram101.com** for the Practice Tests for this Chapter.

Chapter 6. Should the Insanity Defense Be Abolished?

Chapter 7. Are Pretextual Stops by the Police Constitutional?

Majority opinion	In law, a majority opinion is a judicial opinion agreed to by a majority of the members of a court. A majority opinion sets forth the decision of the court and an explanation of the rationale behind the court's decision.
Supreme Court	The supreme court functions as a court of last resort whose rulings cannot be challenged, in some countries, provinces and states. However, in some jurisdictions other phrases are used to describe the highest courts. There are also some jurisdictions where the supreme court is not the highest court.
Criminal law	Criminal law is the body of statutory and common law that deals with crime and the legal punishment of criminal offenses. It is law prohibiting conduct that disrupts social order or challenge's the authority of the state, and consequently deals with matters of significant public concern. In contrast with civil law, actions are pursued by the state rather than private citizens.
Litigation	A lawsuit, also known as litigation, is a criminal or civil action brought before a court in which the party commencing the action, the plaintiff, seeks a legal remedy. Often, one or more defendants are required to answer the plaintiff's complaint.
Probable cause	In United States criminal law, probable cause refers to the standard by which a police officer may make an arrest, conduct a personal or property search or obtain a warrant. It is also used to refer to the standard to which a grand jury believes that a crime has been committed.
Court of Appeal	Court of Appeal is the title of a court which has the power to consider or hear an appeal. A court of appeal is also a superior court.
Constitution	A constitution is a system that establishes the rules and principles that govern an organization or political entity.
Equal protection clause	The Equal Protection Clause, part of the Fourteenth Amendment to the United States Constitution, provides that "no state shall deny to any person within its jurisdiction the equal protection of the laws." The Equal Protection Clause can be seen as an attempt to secure the promise of the United States' professed commitment to the proposition that "all men are created equal" by empowering the judiciary to enforce that principle against the states.
Naturalization	In law, naturalization refers to an act whereby a person acquires a citizenship different from that person's citizenship at birth. Naturalization is most commonly associated with economic migrants or refugees who have immigrated to a country and resided there as aliens, and who have voluntarily and actively chosen to become citizens of that country after meeting specific requirements.
Common law	In common law legal systems, judges have the authority and duty to decide what the law is when there is no other authoritative statement of the law. Once an appellate court has decided what the law is, that precedent tends to bind future decisions of the same appellate court, and binds all lower courts reviewed by that appellate court, when the facts of the case are similar, until there is another authoritative statement of the law.
Case law	Case law the body of judge-made law and legal decisions that interprets prior case law, statutes and other legal authority -- including doctrinal writings by legal scholars such as the Corpus Juris Secundum, Halsbury's Laws of England or the doctrinal writings found in the Recueil Dalloz and law commissions such as the American Law Institute.
Police power	Police power is the capacity of a state to regulate behaviors and enforce order within its territory, often framed in terms of public welfare, security, morality, and safety. Police power is legally considered an inherent right, and is limited only by prohibitions specified in the constitution of a state, making it the most expansive authority exercised by a state.

Go to **Cram101.com** for the Practice Tests for this Chapter.

Chapter 7. Are Pretextual Stops by the Police Constitutional?

Chapter 7. Are Pretextual Stops by the Police Constitutional?

Authoritarianism	Authoritarianism describes a form of social control characterized by strict obedience to the authority of a state or organization, often maintaining and enforcing control through the use of oppressive measures.
Doctrine	Doctrine is a body of axioms fundamental to the exercise of a nation's foreign policy. Hence, doctrine, in this sense, has come to suggest a broad consistency that holds true across a spectrum of acts and actions.
Legislation	Legislation is law which has been promulgated (or "enacted") by a legislature or other governing body. The term may refer to a single law, or the collective body of enacted law, while "statute" is also used to refer to a single law. Before an item of legislation becomes law it may be known as a bill, which is typically also known as "legislation" while it remains under active consideration.
Capital punishment	Capital punishment is the execution of a convicted criminal by the state as punishment for crimes known as capital crimes or capital offences. Historically, the execution of criminals and political opponents was used by nearly all societies—both to punish crime and to suppress political dissent.

Chapter 7. Are Pretextual Stops by the Police Constitutional?

Chapter 8. Do Religious Groups Have a Right to Use Public School Facilities After Hours?

Majority opinion	In law, a majority opinion is a judicial opinion agreed to by a majority of the members of a court. A majority opinion sets forth the decision of the court and an explanation of the rationale behind the court's decision.
Supreme Court	The supreme court functions as a court of last resort whose rulings cannot be challenged, in some countries, provinces and states. However, in some jurisdictions other phrases are used to describe the highest courts. There are also some jurisdictions where the supreme court is not the highest court.
Dissenting opinion	A dissenting opinion is an opinion of one or more judges expressing disagreement with the majority opinion. A dissenting opinion cannot create binding precedent because the holding in the opinion is not the holding of the court in the case.
Establishment clause	The Establishment Clause of the First Amendment to the United States Constitution states that:"Congress shall make no law respecting an establishment of religion" Together with the Free Exercise Clause, these two clauses make up what are commonly known as the religion clauses.
Constitution	A constitution is a system that establishes the rules and principles that govern an organization or political entity.
First Amendment	The First Amendment to the United States Constitution is a part of the United States Bill of Rights. It prohibits the federal legislature from making laws that establish religion or prohibit free exercise of religion, laws that infringe the freedom of
Township	A township is a settlement which has been granted the status and powers of a unit of local government. Specific use of the term to describe political subdivisions has varied by country.
Plaintiff	A plaintiff is the party who initiates a lawsuit before a court. By doing so, the plaintiff seeks a legal remedy, and if successful, the court will issue judgment in favor of the plaintiff and make the appropriate court order .
Welfare	Welfare is financial assistance paid by taxpayers to groups of people who are unable to support themselves, and determined to be able to function more effectively with financial assistance.
Injunction	An injunction is an equitable remedy in the form of a court order, whereby a party is required to do, or to refrain from doing, certain acts. The party that fails to adhere to the injunction faces civil or criminal penalties and may have to pay damages or accept sanctions for failing to follow the court's order. In some cases, breaches of injunctions are considered serious criminal offences that merit arrest and possible prison sentences.
Court of Appeal	Court of Appeal is the title of a court which has the power to consider or hear an appeal. A court of appeal is also a superior court.
Courts of appeals	Courts of Appeals or Court of Appeal is the title of a court which has the power to consider or hear an appeal. A court of appeal is also a superior court
Patriotism	Patriotism denotes positive and supportive attitudes to a 'fatherland', by individuals and groups. The 'fatherland' can be a region or a city, but patriotism usually applies to a nation and/or a nation-state. Patriotism covers such attitudes as: pride in its achievements and culture, the desire to preserve its character and the basis of the culture, and identification with other members of the nation.
Plurality	A plurality, relative majority or simple majority is the largest share of something, which may or may not be considered a majority, i.e. it is the largest group/category, but is not necessarily a majority (more than half). In the U.S., simple majority has another meaning. The plurality voting system, also known as "First past the post", elects the candidate who is

Chapter 8. Do Religious Groups Have a Right to Use Public School Facilities After Hours?

Chapter 8. Do Religious Groups Have a Right to Use Public School Facilities After Hours?

	the stated first choice of the plurality of voters.
Case law	Case law the body of judge-made law and legal decisions that interprets prior case law, statutes and other legal authority -- including doctrinal writings by legal scholars such as the Corpus Juris Secundum, Halsbury's Laws of England or the doctrinal writings found in the Recueil Dalloz and law commissions such as the American Law Institute.
Veto	Veto is used to denote that a certain party has the right to stop unilaterally a certain piece of legislation. A veto gives power, possibly unlimited, to stop changes, but not to adopt them.
Strict scrutiny	Strict scrutiny is the penultimate standard of judicial review used by United States courts reviewing federal law (the most exacting standard, "super strict scrutiny," is used to review prior restraints outside of the Near v. Minnesota exception). Along with the lower standards of rational basis review and intermediate scrutiny, strict scrutiny is part of a hierarchy of standards courts employ to weigh an asserted government interest against a constitutional right or policy that conflicts with the manner in which the interest is being pursued.
Civil liberties	Civil liberties is the name given to freedoms that completely protect the individual from government. Civil liberties set limits for government so that it can not abuse its power and interfere with the lives of its citizens.
Legitimacy	Legitimacy in political science, is the popular acceptance of a governing regime or law as an authority. Where as authority refers to a specific position in an established government, the term legitimacy is used when describing a system of government itself —where "government may be generalized to mean the wider "sphere of influence."
Judiciary	In the law, the judiciary is the system of courts which administer justice in the name of the sovereign or state, a mechanism for the resolution of disputes. The term is also used to refer collectively to the judges, magistrates and other adjudicators who form the core of a judiciary, as well as the support personnel who keep the system running smoothly.
Holocaust	The **Holocaust**, also known as Ha-Shoah, Khurbn or Halokaust, is the term generally used to describe the killing of approximately six million European Jews during World War II, as part of a program of deliberate extermination planned and executed by the National Socialist regime in Germany led by Adolf Hitler.

Go to **Cram101.com** for the Practice Tests for this Chapter.

Chapter 8. Do Religious Groups Have a Right to Use Public School Facilities After Hours?

Chapter 9. Fourth Amendment Search and Seizure Guarantee

Majority opinion	In law, a majority opinion is a judicial opinion agreed to by a majority of the members of a court. A majority opinion sets forth the decision of the court and an explanation of the rationale behind the court's decision.
Supreme Court	The supreme court functions as a court of last resort whose rulings cannot be challenged, in some countries, provinces and states. However, in some jurisdictions other phrases are used to describe the highest courts. There are also some jurisdictions where the supreme court is not the highest court.
Dissenting opinion	A dissenting opinion is an opinion of one or more judges expressing disagreement with the majority opinion. A dissenting opinion cannot create binding precedent because the holding in the opinion is not the holding of the court in the case.
Constitution	A constitution is a system that establishes the rules and principles that govern an organization or political entity.
Search warrant	A search warrant is a written warrant issued by judge or magistrate which authorizes the police to conduct a search of a person or location for evidence of a criminal offense, and seize the evidence. All jurisdictions with a rule of law and a right to privacy put constraints on the rights of police investigators, and typically require search warrants, or an equivalent procedure, for searches within a criminal enquiry.
Probable cause	In United States criminal law, probable cause refers to the standard by which a police officer may make an arrest, conduct a personal or property search or obtain a warrant. It is also used to refer to the standard to which a grand jury believes that a crime has been committed.
Court of Appeal	Court of Appeal is the title of a court which has the power to consider or hear an appeal. A court of appeal is also a superior court.
Case law	Case law the body of judge-made law and legal decisions that interprets prior case law, statutes and other legal authority -- including doctrinal writings by legal scholars such as the Corpus Juris Secundum, Halsbury's Laws of England or the doctrinal writings found in the Recueil Dalloz and law commissions such as the American Law Institute.
Doctrine	Doctrine is a body of axioms fundamental to the exercise of a nation's foreign policy. Hence, doctrine, in this sense, has come to suggest a broad consistency that holds true across a spectrum of acts and actions.
Concurrence	Concurrence is a legal term, from Western jurisprudence, referring to the apparent need to prove the simultaneous occurrence of both actus reus ("guilty action") and mens rea ("guilty mind"), to constitute a crime; except in crimes of strict liability.
Common law	In common law legal systems, judges have the authority and duty to decide what the law is when there is no other authoritative statement of the law. Once an appellate court has decided what the law is, that precedent tends to bind future decisions of the same appellate court, and binds all lower courts reviewed by that appellate court, when the facts of the case are similar, until there is another authoritative statement of the law.
Public interest	The public interest refers to the "common well-being" or "general welfare." The public interest is central to policy debates, politics, democracy and the nature of government itself. While nearly everyone claims that aiding the common well-being or general welfare is positive, there is little, if any, consensus on what exactly constitutes the public interest.
Litigation	A lawsuit, also known as litigation, is a criminal or civil action brought before a court in which the party commencing the action, the plaintiff, seeks a legal remedy. Often, one or more defendants are required to answer the plaintiff's complaint.
Judicial	Judicial restraint is a theory of judicial interpretation that encourages judges to limit the

Chapter 9. Fourth Amendment Search and Seizure Guarantee

Chapter 9. Fourth Amendment Search and Seizure Guarantee

restraint	exercise of their own power. It asserts that judges should hesitate to strike down laws unless they are obviously unconstitutional.[1] It is sometimes regarded as the opposite of judicial activism.
Courts of appeals	Courts of Appeals or Court of Appeal is the title of a court which has the power to consider or hear an appeal. A court of appeal is also a superior court

Go to **Cram101.com** for the Practice Tests for this Chapter.

Chapter 9. Fourth Amendment Search and Seizure Guarantee

Chapter 10. Laws Requiring Schools and Libraries to Filter Internet Access

Majority opinion	In law, a majority opinion is a judicial opinion agreed to by a majority of the members of a court. A majority opinion sets forth the decision of the court and an explanation of the rationale behind the court's decision.
Supreme Court	The supreme court functions as a court of last resort whose rulings cannot be challenged, in some countries, provinces and states. However, in some jurisdictions other phrases are used to describe the highest courts. There are also some jurisdictions where the supreme court is not the highest court.
Dissenting opinion	A dissenting opinion is an opinion of one or more judges expressing disagreement with the majority opinion. A dissenting opinion cannot create binding precedent because the holding in the opinion is not the holding of the court in the case.
First Amendment	The First Amendment to the United States Constitution is a part of the United States Bill of Rights. It prohibits the federal legislature from making laws that establish religion or prohibit free exercise of religion, laws that infringe the freedom of
World Wide Web	World Wide Web is a system of interlinked, hypertext documents accessed via the Internet. With a Web browser, a user views Web pages that may contain text, images, and other multimedia and navigates between them using hyperlinks.
Pornography	Pornography, in its broadest state, the explicit representation of the human body or sexual activity with the goal of sexual arousal. It is similar to erotica, which is the use of sexually-arousing imagery used mainly for artistic purpose.
Legislation	Legislation is law which has been promulgated (or "enacted") by a legislature or other governing body. The term may refer to a single law, or the collective body of enacted law, while "statute" is also used to refer to a single law. Before an item of legislation becomes law it may be known as a bill, which is typically also known as "legislation" while it remains under active consideration.
Civil liberties	Civil liberties is the name given to freedoms that completely protect the individual from government. Civil liberties set limits for government so that it can not abuse its power and interfere with the lives of its citizens.
Coalition	A coalition is an alliance among entities, during which they cooperate in joint action, each in their own self-interest. This alliance may be temporary or a matter of convenience. A coalition government, in a parliamentary system, is a government composed of a coalition of parties.
Fiscal Year	Fiscal year is a 12-month period used for calculating annual financial statements in businesses and other organizations.
Strict scrutiny	Strict scrutiny is the penultimate standard of judicial review used by United States courts reviewing federal law (the most exacting standard, "super strict scrutiny," is used to review prior restraints outside of the Near v. Minnesota exception). Along with the lower standards of rational basis review and intermediate scrutiny, strict scrutiny is part of a hierarchy of standards courts employ to weigh an asserted government interest against a constitutional right or policy that conflicts with the manner in which the interest is being pursued.
Jurisdiction	In law, jurisdiction is the practical authority granted to a formally constituted legal body or to a political leader to deal with and make pronouncements on legal matters and, by implication, to administer justice within a defined area of responsibility.
Bill of Rights	A bill of rights is a list or summary of which is considered important and essential by a group of people. The purpose of these bills is to protect those rights against infringement by other people and the government.
Mandate	In international law, a mandate is a binding obligation issued from an inter-governmental

Go to **Cram101.com** for the Practice Tests for this Chapter.

Chapter 10. Laws Requiring Schools and Libraries to Filter Internet Access

Chapter 10. Laws Requiring Schools and Libraries to Filter Internet Access

	organization like the United Nations to a country which is bound to follow the instructions of the organization.
Solicitor general	The United States Solicitor General is the individual appointed to argue for the Government of the United States in front of the Supreme Court of the United States, when the government is party to a case.
Constitution	A constitution is a system that establishes the rules and principles that govern an organization or political entity.
Doctrine	Doctrine is a body of axioms fundamental to the exercise of a nation's foreign policy. Hence, doctrine, in this sense, has come to suggest a broad consistency that holds true across a spectrum of acts and actions.
Entitlement	Entitlement is a guarantee of access to benefits because of rights, or by agreement through law. It can also refer, in a more casual sense to someone's belief that they are deserving of some particular reward or benefit. It is often used as a negative term in popular parlance The legal term, however, carries no value judgment, it simply denotes a right granted. It was issued in 1965 by Presidents Johnson's administration.
Subsidies	In economics, a subsidies is a kind of financial government assistance, such as a grant, tax break, or trade barrier, in order to encourage the production or purchase of a good. The term subsidy may also refer to assistance granted by others, such as individuals or non-government institutions, although this is more commonly described as charity.
Representation	In politics, representation describes how residents of a country are empowered in the government. Representation usually refers to representative democracies, where elected representatives speak for their constituents in the legislature. Generally, only citizens are granted representation in the government in the form of voting rights, however some democracies have extended this right further.
Corporation	A corporation is an artificial legal entity which, while made up of a number of natural persons or other legal entities, has a separate legal identity from them. As a legal entity the corporation receives legal rights and duties
Welfare	Welfare is financial assistance paid by taxpayers to groups of people who are unable to support themselves, and determined to be able to function more effectively with financial assistance.
Consortium	A consortium is an association of two or more individuals, companies, organizations or governments with the objective of participating in a common activity or pooling their resources for achieving a common goal
Prior restraint	Prior restraint is a legal term referring to a government's actions that prevent materials from being published. Censorship that requires a person to seek governmental permission in the form of a license or imprimatur before publishing anything constitutes prior restraint every time permission is denied.
State action	A state action is a term used in United States civil rights law to describe a person who is acting on behalf of a governmental body, and is therefore subject to regulation under the United States bill of rights including the First, Fifth and Fourteenth Amendments, which prohibit the federal and state governments from violating certain rights and freedoms.
Case law	Case law the body of judge-made law and legal decisions that interprets prior case law, statutes and other legal authority -- including doctrinal writings by legal scholars such as the Corpus Juris Secundum, Halsbury's Laws of England or the doctrinal writings found in the Recueil Dalloz and law commissions such as the American Law Institute.
Plurality	A plurality, relative majority or simple majority is the largest share of something, which

Go to **Cram101.com** for the Practice Tests for this Chapter.

Chapter 10. Laws Requiring Schools and Libraries to Filter Internet Access

Chapter 10. Laws Requiring Schools and Libraries to Filter Internet Access

	may or may not be considered a majority, i.e. it is the largest group/category, but is not necessarily a majority (more than half). In the U.S., simple majority has another meaning. The plurality voting system, also known as "First past the post", elects the candidate who is the stated first choice of the plurality of voters.
Freedom of speech	Freedom of speech is the concept of the inherent human right to voice one's opinion publicly without fear of censorship or punishment.
Feminism	Feminism is the name of a number of social, cultural and political movements, theories and moral philosophies that are concerned cultural, political and economic practices and inequalities that discriminate against women.

Chapter 10. Laws Requiring Schools and Libraries to Filter Internet Access

Chapter 11. Is It Constitutional to Impose the Death Penalty on the Mentally Retarded?

Majority opinion	In law, a majority opinion is a judicial opinion agreed to by a majority of the members of a court. A majority opinion sets forth the decision of the court and an explanation of the rationale behind the court's decision.
Supreme Court	The supreme court functions as a court of last resort whose rulings cannot be challenged, in some countries, provinces and states. However, in some jurisdictions other phrases are used to describe the highest courts. There are also some jurisdictions where the supreme court is not the highest court.
American Bar Association	American Bar Association is a voluntary bar association of lawyers and law students, which is not specific to any jurisdiction in the United States.
Amicus curiae	Amicus curiae, is a legal Latin phrase, literally translated as "friend of the court", that refers to someone, not a party to a case, who volunteers to offer information on a point of law or some other aspect of the case to assist the court in deciding a matter before it. The information may be a legal opinion in the form of a brief - testimony that has not been solicited by any of the parties - or a learned treatise on a matter that bears on the case. The decision whether to admit the information lies with the discretion of the court.
Constitution	A constitution is a system that establishes the rules and principles that govern an organization or political entity.
Eighth Amendment	The Eighth Amendment of the United States Constitution, which is part of the U.S. Bill of Rights, prohibits excessive bail or fines, as well as cruel and unusual punishment. The phrases employed are taken from the English Bill of Rights.
Capital punishment	Capital punishment is the execution of a convicted criminal by the state as punishment for crimes known as capital crimes or capital offences. Historically, the execution of criminals and political opponents was used by nearly all societies—both to punish crime and to suppress political dissent.
Cruel and unusual punishment	The statement that the government shall not inflict cruel and unusual punishment for crimes is found in the English Bill of Rights signed in 1689 by King William III and Queen Mary II who were then the joint rulers of England following the 'Glorious Revolution' of 1688. These exact words later appeared in the Eighth Amendment to the United States Constitution (1787).
Human rights	Human rights refers to universal rights of people regardless of jurisdiction or other factors, such as ethnicity, age, nationality, sexual orientation or religion.
Due process	In United States law, adopted from English Law, due process is the principle that the government must normally respect all of a person's legal rights instead of just some or most of those legal rights when the government deprives a person of life, liberty, or property. Due process has also been frequently interpreted as placing limitations on laws and legal proceedings, in order for judges instead of legislators to guarantee fundamental fairness, justice, and liberty.
United Nations	The United Nations is an international organization whose stated aims are to facilitate co-operation in international law, international security, economic development, social progress and human rights issues.
Trial court	A trial court is the court in which most civil or criminal cases begin. Not all cases are heard in a trial court; some cases may begin in inferior limited jurisdiction bodies such as the case of the jurisdiction of an administrative body that has been created by statute to make some kind of binding determination under the law and were simplified procedural practices may apply similar to arbitration.
Bill of Rights	A bill of rights is a list or summary of which is considered important and essential by a group of people. The purpose of these bills is to protect those rights against infringement

Chapter 11. Is It Constitutional to Impose the Death Penalty on the Mentally Retarded?

Chapter 11. Is It Constitutional to Impose the Death Penalty on the Mentally Retarded?

	by other people and the government.
Common law	In common law legal systems, judges have the authority and duty to decide what the law is when there is no other authoritative statement of the law. Once an appellate court has decided what the law is, that precedent tends to bind future decisions of the same appellate court, and binds all lower courts reviewed by that appellate court, when the facts of the case are similar, until there is another authoritative statement of the law.
Legislation	Legislation is law which has been promulgated (or "enacted") by a legislature or other governing body. The term may refer to a single law, or the collective body of enacted law, while "statute" is also used to refer to a single law. Before an item of legislation becomes law it may be known as a bill, which is typically also known as "legislation" while it remains under active consideration.
Treason	In law, treason is the crime of disloyalty to one's nation. A person who betrays the nation of their citizenship and/or reneges on an oath of loyalty and in some way willfully cooperates with an enemy.
Criminal law	Criminal law is the body of statutory and common law that deals with crime and the legal punishment of criminal offenses. It is law prohibiting conduct that disrupts social order or challenge's the authority of the state, and consequently deals with matters of significant public concern. In contrast with civil law, actions are pursued by the state rather than private citizens.
Plurality	A plurality, relative majority or simple majority is the largest share of something, which may or may not be considered a majority, i.e. it is the largest group/category, but is not necessarily a majority (more than half). In the U.S., simple majority has another meaning. The plurality voting system, also known as "First past the post", elects the candidate who is the stated first choice of the plurality of voters.
Representation	In politics, representation describes how residents of a country are empowered in the government. Representation usually refers to representative democracies, where elected representatives speak for their constituents in the legislature. Generally, only citizens are granted representation in the government in the form of voting rights, however some democracies have extended this right further.
Attorney General	The Attorney General is the main legal adviser to the government, and in some jurisdictions may in addition have executive responsibility for law enforcement or responsibility for public prosecutions.
Miranda rights	Miranda rights were mandated by the 1966 United States Supreme Court decision in the case of Miranda v. Arizona as a means of protecting a criminal suspect's Fifth Amendment right to avoid coercive self-incrimination.
Reprieve	Reprieve is the name of a number of not-for-profit organizations around the world which work against the death penalty, with a particular focus on legal support for those facing the death penalty.
Legislature	A legislature is a type of representative deliberative assembly with the power to adopt laws. In presidential systems of government, the legislature is considered a power branch which is equal to, and independent of, the executive.
Treaty	A treaty is an agreement under international law entered into by actors in international law, namely states and international organizations. Under United States constitutional law, only a treaty that has achieved advice and consent of two-thirds of the Senate present is properly designated as a treaty.

Go to **Cram101.com** for the Practice Tests for this Chapter.

Chapter 11. Is It Constitutional to Impose the Death Penalty on the Mentally Retarded?

Chapter 12. Is a Sentence of Life in Prison for Stealing $150 Constitutional?

Majority opinion	In law, a majority opinion is a judicial opinion agreed to by a majority of the members of a court. A majority opinion sets forth the decision of the court and an explanation of the rationale behind the court's decision.
Attorney General	The Attorney General is the main legal adviser to the government, and in some jurisdictions may in addition have executive responsibility for law enforcement or responsibility for public prosecutions.
Supreme Court	The supreme court functions as a court of last resort whose rulings cannot be challenged, in some countries, provinces and states. However, in some jurisdictions other phrases are used to describe the highest courts. There are also some jurisdictions where the supreme court is not the highest court.
Dissenting opinion	A dissenting opinion is an opinion of one or more judges expressing disagreement with the majority opinion. A dissenting opinion cannot create binding precedent because the holding in the opinion is not the holding of the court in the case.
Eighth Amendment	The Eighth Amendment of the United States Constitution, which is part of the U.S. Bill of Rights, prohibits excessive bail or fines, as well as cruel and unusual punishment. The phrases employed are taken from the English Bill of Rights.
Cruel and unusual punishment	The statement that the government shall not inflict cruel and unusual punishment for crimes is found in the English Bill of Rights signed in 1689 by King William III and Queen Mary II who were then the joint rulers of England following the 'Glorious Revolution' of 1688. These exact words later appeared in the Eighth Amendment to the United States Constitution (1787).
Court of Appeal	Court of Appeal is the title of a court which has the power to consider or hear an appeal. A court of appeal is also a superior court.
Probation	Probation is the suspension of a jail sentence - the criminal who is "on probation" has been convicted of a crime, but instead of serving jail time, has been found by the Court to be amenable to probation and will be returned to the community for a period in which they will have to abide to certain conditions set forth by the Court under the supervision of a probation officer.
Misdemeanor	A misdemeanor in many common law legal systems, is a "lesser" criminal act. Misdemeanors are generally punished less severely than felonies; but theoretically more so than administrative infractions (also known as regulatory offenses).
Trial court	A trial court is the court in which most civil or criminal cases begin. Not all cases are heard in a trial court; some cases may begin in inferior limited jurisdiction bodies such as the case of the jurisdiction of an administrative body that has been created by statute to make some kind of binding determination under the law and were simplified procedural practices may apply similar to arbitration.
Regime	A regime is the set of rules, both formal and informal that regulate the operation of government and its interactions with the economy and society.
Habeas corpus	In common law, habeas corpus is the name of a legal action or writ by means of which detainees can seek relief from unlawful imprisonment. The writ of habeas corpus has historically been an important instrument for the safeguarding of individual freedom against arbitrary state action.
Constitution	A constitution is a system that establishes the rules and principles that govern an organization or political entity.
Writ	In law, a writ is a formal written order issued by a body with administrative or judicial jurisdiction. In modern usage, this public body is normally a court. Warrants, prerogative

Chapter 12. Is a Sentence of Life in Prison for Stealing $150 Constitutional?

Chapter 12. Is a Sentence of Life in Prison for Stealing $150 Constitutional?

	writs, and subpoenas are types of writs, but there are many others.
Adjudication	Adjudication is the legal process by which an arbiter or judge reviews evidence and argumentation including legal reasoning set forth by opposing parties or litigants to come to a decision which determines rights and obligations between the parties involved.
Constitutional law	Constitutional law is the study of foundational or basic laws of nation states and other political organizations. Constitutions are the framework for government and may limit or define the authority and procedure of political bodies to execute new laws and regulations.
Indictment	In the common law legal system, an indictment is a formal charge of having committed a most serious criminal offense. In those jurisdictions which retain the concept of a felony, the serious criminal offense would be a felony; those jurisdictions which have abolished the concept of a felony often substitute instead the concept of an indictable offence, i.e. an offense which requires an indictment.
Deterrence	Deterrence theory is a military strategy developed after and used throughout the Cold War and current times. It is especially relevant with regard to the use of nuclear weapons, and figures prominently on current United States foreign policy regarding the development of nuclear technology in North Korea and Iran.
Jurisdiction	In law, jurisdiction is the practical authority granted to a formally constituted legal body or to a political leader to deal with and make pronouncements on legal matters and, by implication, to administer justice within a defined area of responsibility.
Legislature	A legislature is a type of representative deliberative assembly with the power to adopt laws. In presidential systems of government, the legislature is considered a power branch which is equal to, and independent of, the executive.
Double jeopardy	Double jeopardy is a procedural defense that forbids a defendant from being tried a second time for the same crime.
Legitimacy	Legitimacy in political science, is the popular acceptance of a governing regime or law as an authority. Where as authority refers to a specific position in an established government, the term legitimacy is used when describing a system of government itself —where "government may be generalized to mean the wider "sphere of influence."
Criminal law	Criminal law is the body of statutory and common law that deals with crime and the legal punishment of criminal offenses. It is law prohibiting conduct that disrupts social order or challenge's the authority of the state, and consequently deals with matters of significant public concern. In contrast with civil law, actions are pursued by the state rather than private citizens.
Democracy	Democracy is a form of government in which supreme power is vested in the people and exercised by them directly or indirectly through a system of representation usually involving periodic free elections.
Litigation	A lawsuit, also known as litigation, is a criminal or civil action brought before a court in which the party commencing the action, the plaintiff, seeks a legal remedy. Often, one or more defendants are required to answer the plaintiff's complaint.

Chapter 12. Is a Sentence of Life in Prison for Stealing $150 Constitutional?

Chapter 13. Drug Use Testing of Students Who Participate in Extracurricular Activities

Majority opinion	In law, a majority opinion is a judicial opinion agreed to by a majority of the members of a court. A majority opinion sets forth the decision of the court and an explanation of the rationale behind the court's decision.
Supreme Court	The supreme court functions as a court of last resort whose rulings cannot be challenged, in some countries, provinces and states. However, in some jurisdictions other phrases are used to describe the highest courts. There are also some jurisdictions where the supreme court is not the highest court.
Dissenting opinion	A dissenting opinion is an opinion of one or more judges expressing disagreement with the majority opinion. A dissenting opinion cannot create binding precedent because the holding in the opinion is not the holding of the court in the case.
Initiative	In political science, the initiative provides a means by which a petition signed by a certain minimum number of registered voters can force a public vote on a proposed statute, constitutional amendment, charter amendment or ordinance, or, in its minimal form, to simply oblige the executive or legislative bodies to consider the subject by submitting it to the order of the day.
Corporation	A corporation is an artificial legal entity which, while made up of a number of natural persons or other legal entities, has a separate legal identity from them. As a legal entity the corporation receives legal rights and duties
Court of Appeal	Court of Appeal is the title of a court which has the power to consider or hear an appeal. A court of appeal is also a superior court.
Probable cause	In United States criminal law, probable cause refers to the standard by which a police officer may make an arrest, conduct a personal or property search or obtain a warrant. It is also used to refer to the standard to which a grand jury believes that a crime has been committed.
Constitution	A constitution is a system that establishes the rules and principles that govern an organization or political entity.
Regime	A regime is the set of rules, both formal and informal that regulate the operation of government and its interactions with the economy and society.
National security	National security refers to the requirement to maintain the survival of the nation-state through the use of economic, military and political power and the exercise of diplomacy.
Bench trial	A bench trial in the U.S. is a trial before a judge in which the right to a jury trial has been waived by the necessary parties. In the case of a criminal trial, in most states the criminal defendant alone has the ability to waive the right to a jury. In a civil trial, one of the parties must request a jury trial otherwise a bench trial will result.
Per curiam	A per curiam is a ruling handed down by a court with multiple judges in which the decision was made by the court acting as a whole, as opposed to statements made by individual judges. The literal meaning of this legal term is "by the court".
Amicus curiae	Amicus curiae, is a legal Latin phrase, literally translated as "friend of the court", that refers to someone, not a party to a case, who volunteers to offer information on a point of law or some other aspect of the case to assist the court in deciding a matter before it. The information may be a legal opinion in the form of a brief - testimony that has not been solicited by any of the parties - or a learned treatise on a matter that bears on the case. The decision whether to admit the information lies with the discretion of the court.
Deterrence	Deterrence theory is a military strategy developed after and used throughout the Cold War and current times. It is especially relevant with regard to the use of nuclear weapons, and figures prominently on current United States foreign policy regarding the development of

Go to **Cram101.com** for the Practice Tests for this Chapter.

Chapter 13. Drug Use Testing of Students Who Participate in Extracurricular Activities

Chapter 13. Drug Use Testing of Students Who Participate in Extracurricular Activities

	nuclear technology in North Korea and Iran.
Case law	Case law the body of judge-made law and legal decisions that interprets prior case law, statutes and other legal authority -- including doctrinal writings by legal scholars such as the Corpus Juris Secundum, Halsbury's Laws of England or the doctrinal writings found in the Recueil Dalloz and law commissions such as the American Law Institute.
Citizenship	Citizenship is membership in a political community and carries with it rights to political participation; a person having such membership is a citizen. It is largely coterminous with nationality, although it is possible to have a nationality without being a citizen ; it is also possible to have political rights without being a national of a state.
Concurring opinion	In law, a concurring opinion is a written opinion by some of the judges of a court which agrees with the majority of the court but might arrive there in a different manner. In a concurring opinion, the author agrees with the decision of the court but normally states reasons different from those in the court opinion as the basis for his or her decision. When no absolute majority of the court can agree on the basis for deciding the case, the decision of the court may be contained in a number of concurring opinions, and the concurring opinion joined by the greatest number of jurists is referred to as the plurality opinion.
First Amendment	The First Amendment to the United States Constitution is a part of the United States Bill of Rights. It prohibits the federal legislature from making laws that establish religion or prohibit free exercise of religion, laws that infringe the freedom of

Chapter 13. Drug Use Testing of Students Who Participate in Extracurricular Activities

Chapter 14. Can Companies That Lie About Their Business Practices

Majority opinion	In law, a majority opinion is a judicial opinion agreed to by a majority of the members of a court. A majority opinion sets forth the decision of the court and an explanation of the rationale behind the court's decision.
Supreme Court	The supreme court functions as a court of last resort whose rulings cannot be challenged, in some countries, provinces and states. However, in some jurisdictions other phrases are used to describe the highest courts. There are also some jurisdictions where the supreme court is not the highest court.
Dissenting opinion	A dissenting opinion is an opinion of one or more judges expressing disagreement with the majority opinion. A dissenting opinion cannot create binding precedent because the holding in the opinion is not the holding of the court in the case.
First Amendment	The First Amendment to the United States Constitution is a part of the United States Bill of Rights. It prohibits the federal legislature from making laws that establish religion or prohibit free exercise of religion, laws that infringe the freedom of
Legitimacy	Legitimacy in political science, is the popular acceptance of a governing regime or law as an authority. Where as authority refers to a specific position in an established government, the term legitimacy is used when describing a system of government itself —where "government may be generalized to mean the wider "sphere of influence."
Case law	Case law the body of judge-made law and legal decisions that interprets prior case law, statutes and other legal authority -- including doctrinal writings by legal scholars such as the Corpus Juris Secundum, Halsbury's Laws of England or the doctrinal writings found in the Recueil Dalloz and law commissions such as the American Law Institute.
Globalization	Globalization is an umbrella term and is perhaps best understood as a unitary process inclusive of many sub-processes (such as enhanced economic interdependence, increased cultural influence, rapid advances of information technology, and novel governance and geopolitical challenges) that are increasingly binding people and the biosphere more tightly into one global system.
Democracy	Democracy is a form of government in which supreme power is vested in the people and exercised by them directly or indirectly through a system of representation usually involving periodic free elections.
Sovereignty	Sovereignty is the exclusive right to exercise supreme political authority over a geographic region, group of people, or oneself. The source or justification of sovereignty ("by God" or "by people") must be distinguished from its exercise by branches of government. In democratic states, sovereignty is held by the people.
Censorship	Censorship is the removal and withholding of information from the public by a controlling group or body. Typically censorship is done by governments, religious groups, or the mass media, although other forms of censorship exist. The withholding of official secrets, commercial secrets, intellectual property, and privileged lawyer-client communication is not usually described as censorship when it remains within reasonable bounds.
Plaintiff	A plaintiff is the party who initiates a lawsuit before a court. By doing so, the plaintiff seeks a legal remedy, and if successful, the court will issue judgment in favor of the plaintiff and make the appropriate court order .
Corporation	A corporation is an artificial legal entity which, while made up of a number of natural persons or other legal entities, has a separate legal identity from them. As a legal entity the corporation receives legal rights and duties
Constitution	A constitution is a system that establishes the rules and principles that govern an organization or political entity.

Go to Cram101.com for the Practice Tests for this Chapter.

Chapter 14. Can Companies That Lie About Their Business Practices

Chapter 14. Can Companies That Lie About Their Business Practices

Bill of Rights	A bill of rights is a list or summary of which is considered important and essential by a group of people. The purpose of these bills is to protect those rights against infringement by other people and the government.
Freedom of speech	Freedom of speech is the concept of the inherent human right to voice one's opinion publicly without fear of censorship or punishment.
Due process	In United States law, adopted from English Law, due process is the principle that the government must normally respect all of a person's legal rights instead of just some or most of those legal rights when the government deprives a person of life, liberty, or property. Due process has also been frequently interpreted as placing limitations on laws and legal proceedings, in order for judges instead of legislators to guarantee fundamental fairness, justice, and liberty.
Strict scrutiny	Strict scrutiny is the penultimate standard of judicial review used by United States courts reviewing federal law (the most exacting standard, "super strict scrutiny," is used to review prior restraints outside of the Near v. Minnesota exception). Along with the lower standards of rational basis review and intermediate scrutiny, strict scrutiny is part of a hierarchy of standards courts employ to weigh an asserted government interest against a constitutional right or policy that conflicts with the manner in which the interest is being pursued.
Trade association	Trade association is generally a public relations organization founded and funded by corporations that operate in a specific industry. Its purpose is generally to promote the industry through PR activities such as advertising, education, political donations, lobbying and publishing.
Civil rights	Civil rights are the protections and privileges of personal power given to all citizens by law. Civil rights are distinguished from "human rights" or "natural rights", also called "our God-given rights". They are rights that are bestowed by nations on those within their territorial boundaries, while natural or human rights are rights that many scholars claim should belong to all people.
Public interest	The public interest refers to the "common well-being" or "general welfare." The public interest is central to policy debates, politics, democracy and the nature of government itself. While nearly everyone claims that aiding the common well-being or general welfare is positive, there is little, if any, consensus on what exactly constitutes the public interest.
Doctrine	Doctrine is a body of axioms fundamental to the exercise of a nation's foreign policy. Hence, doctrine, in this sense, has come to suggest a broad consistency that holds true across a spectrum of acts and actions.
Court of Appeal	Court of Appeal is the title of a court which has the power to consider or hear an appeal. A court of appeal is also a superior court.
Actual malice	Actual malice in United States law is a condition required to establish libel against public figures and is defined as "knowledge that the information was false" or that it was published "with reckless disregard of whether it was false or not."
Trial court	A trial court is the court in which most civil or criminal cases begin. Not all cases are heard in a trial court; some cases may begin in inferior limited jurisdiction bodies such as the case of the jurisdiction of an administrative body that has been created by statute to make some kind of binding determination under the law and were simplified procedural practices may apply similar to arbitration.
Hierarchy	Hierarchy is a system of ranking and organizing things or people, where each element of the system is subordinate to a single other element.
Representation	In politics, representation describes how residents of a country are empowered in the government. Representation usually refers to representative democracies, where elected

Chapter 14. Can Companies That Lie About Their Business Practices

Chapter 14. Can Companies That Lie About Their Business Practices

	representatives speak for their constituents in the legislature. Generally, only citizens are granted representation in the government in the form of voting rights, however some democracies have extended this right further.
Legislation	Legislation is law which has been promulgated (or "enacted") by a legislature or other governing body. The term may refer to a single law, or the collective body of enacted law, while "statute" is also used to refer to a single law. Before an item of legislation becomes law it may be known as a bill, which is typically also known as "legislation" while it remains under active consideration.
Political philosophy	Political philosophy is the study of fundamental questions about the state, government, politics, liberty, justice, property, rights, law and the enforcement of a legal code by authority: what they are, why they are needed, what makes a government legitimate, what rights and freedoms it should protect and why, what form it should take and why, what the law is, and what duties citizens owe to a legitimate government, if any, and when it may be legitimately overthrown—if ever.

Chapter 14. Can Companies That Lie About Their Business Practices

Chapter 15. Are Blanket Prohibitions on Cross Burnings Unconstitutional?

Majority opinion	In law, a majority opinion is a judicial opinion agreed to by a majority of the members of a court. A majority opinion sets forth the decision of the court and an explanation of the rationale behind the court's decision.
Supreme Court	The supreme court functions as a court of last resort whose rulings cannot be challenged, in some countries, provinces and states. However, in some jurisdictions other phrases are used to describe the highest courts. There are also some jurisdictions where the supreme court is not the highest court.
Dissenting opinion	A dissenting opinion is an opinion of one or more judges expressing disagreement with the majority opinion. A dissenting opinion cannot create binding precedent because the holding in the opinion is not the holding of the court in the case.
Symbolic speech	Symbolic speech is a legal term for an action that expresses an opinion or idea non-verbally. Because it involves action and not simply written or spoken words, this form of expression is subject to more government regulation.
Terrorism	As a form of unconventional warfare, terrorism is sometimes used when attempting to force political change by: convincing a government or population to agree to demands to avoid future harm or fear of harm, destabilization of an existing government, motivating a disgruntled population to join an uprizing, escalating a conflict in the hopes of disrupting the status quo, expressing a grievance, or drawing attention to a cause.
Legislature	A legislature is a type of representative deliberative assembly with the power to adopt laws. In presidential systems of government, the legislature is considered a power branch which is equal to, and independent of, the executive.
Commonwealth	Commonwealth originally meant a state governed for the common good as opposed to an authoritarian state governed for the benefit of a given class of owners. Today the term is more general and means a political community.
First Amendment	The First Amendment to the United States Constitution is a part of the United States Bill of Rights. It prohibits the federal legislature from making laws that establish religion or prohibit free exercise of religion, laws that infringe the freedom of
Trial court	A trial court is the court in which most civil or criminal cases begin. Not all cases are heard in a trial court; some cases may begin in inferior limited jurisdiction bodies such as the case of the jurisdiction of an administrative body that has been created by statute to make some kind of binding determination under the law and were simplified procedural practices may apply similar to arbitration.
Court of Appeal	Court of Appeal is the title of a court which has the power to consider or hear an appeal. A court of appeal is also a superior court.
Reconstruction	Reconstruction was the attempts from 1865 to 1877 in U.S. history to resolve the issues of the American Civil War, when both the Confederacy and slavery were destroyed. Reconstruction addressed the return of the Southern states that had seceded, the status of ex-Confederate leaders, and the Constitutional and legal status of the African-American Freedmen.
Ideology	An ideology is an organized collection of ideas. The word ideology was coined by Count Antoine Destutt de Tracy in the late 18th century to define a "science of ideas." An ideology can be thought of as a comprehensive vision, as a way of looking at things, as in common sense and several philosophical tendencies, or a set of ideas proposed by the dominant class of a society to all members of this society.
Civil rights	Civil rights are the protections and privileges of personal power given to all citizens by law. Civil rights are distinguished from "human rights" or "natural rights", also called "our God-given rights". They are rights that are bestowed by nations on those within their territorial boundaries, while natural or human rights are rights that many scholars claim

Go to **Cram101.com** for the Practice Tests for this Chapter.

Chapter 15. Are Blanket Prohibitions on Cross Burnings Unconstitutional?

Chapter 15. Are Blanket Prohibitions on Cross Burnings Unconstitutional?

	should belong to all people.
Civil rights movement	The civil rights movement was a concentrated period of time around the world of approximately one generation (1954–1980) wherein there was much worldwide civil unrest and popular rebellion. The process of moving toward equality under the law was long and tenuous in many countries, and most of these movements did not achieve or fully achieve their objectives.
Constitution	A constitution is a system that establishes the rules and principles that govern an organization or political entity.
Freedom of speech	Freedom of speech is the concept of the inherent human right to voice one's opinion publicly without fear of censorship or punishment.
Doctrine	Doctrine is a body of axioms fundamental to the exercise of a nation's foreign policy. Hence, doctrine, in this sense, has come to suggest a broad consistency that holds true across a spectrum of acts and actions.
Free Press	Free Press is a non-partisan, non-profit organization founded by media critic Robert McChesney to promote more democratic media policy in the United States.
Solicitor general	The United States Solicitor General is the individual appointed to argue for the Government of the United States in front of the Supreme Court of the United States, when the government is party to a case.
Conservativism	Conservativism is a relativistic term used to describe political philosophies that favor traditional values, where "tradition" refers to religious, cultural, or nationally defined beliefs and customs.
Delegate	A delegate is an individual or a member of a group called at the interests of a larger organization at a meeting of some kind. In order to avoid the principal-agent problem, it is generally important to the organization to take steps to ensure that the delegate does not have a conflict of interest.
Law and order	In politics, law and order refers to a political platform which supports a strict criminal justice system, especially in relation to violent crime and property crime, through harsher criminal penalties. These penalties may include longer terms of imprisonment, mandatory sentencing, and in some countries, capital punishment.
Plurality	A plurality, relative majority or simple majority is the largest share of something, which may or may not be considered a majority, i.e. it is the largest group/category, but is not necessarily a majority (more than half). In the U.S., simple majority has another meaning. The plurality voting system, also known as "First past the post", elects the candidate who is the stated first choice of the plurality of voters.
Rule of law	The rule of law is the principle that governmental authority is legitimately exercised only in accordance with written, publicly disclosed laws adopted and enforced in accordance with established procedure.
Due process	In United States law, adopted from English Law, due process is the principle that the government must normally respect all of a person's legal rights instead of just some or most of those legal rights when the government deprives a person of life, liberty, or property. Due process has also been frequently interpreted as placing limitations on laws and legal proceedings, in order for judges instead of legislators to guarantee fundamental fairness, justice, and liberty.
Pornography	Pornography, in its broadest state, the explicit representation of the human body or sexual activity with the goal of sexual arousal. It is similar to erotica, which is the use of sexually-arousing imagery used mainly for artistic purpose.
Mandate	In international law, a mandate is a binding obligation issued from an inter-governmental

Go to Cram101.com for the Practice Tests for this Chapter.

Chapter 15. Are Blanket Prohibitions on Cross Burnings Unconstitutional?

Chapter 15. Are Blanket Prohibitions on Cross Burnings Unconstitutional?

	organization like the United Nations to a country which is bound to follow the instructions of the organization.
Coalition	A coalition is an alliance among entities, during which they cooperate in joint action, each in their own self-interest. This alliance may be temporary or a matter of convenience. A coalition government, in a parliamentary system, is a government composed of a coalition of parties.

Chapter 15. Are Blanket Prohibitions on Cross Burnings Unconstitutional?

Chapter 16. Are Laws Criminalizing Homosexual Conduct Unconstitutional?

Majority opinion	In law, a majority opinion is a judicial opinion agreed to by a majority of the members of a court. A majority opinion sets forth the decision of the court and an explanation of the rationale behind the court's decision.
Supreme Court	The supreme court functions as a court of last resort whose rulings cannot be challenged, in some countries, provinces and states. However, in some jurisdictions other phrases are used to describe the highest courts. There are also some jurisdictions where the supreme court is not the highest court.
Dissenting opinion	A dissenting opinion is an opinion of one or more judges expressing disagreement with the majority opinion. A dissenting opinion cannot create binding precedent because the holding in the opinion is not the holding of the court in the case.
Due process	In United States law, adopted from English Law, due process is the principle that the government must normally respect all of a person's legal rights instead of just some or most of those legal rights when the government deprives a person of life, liberty, or property. Due process has also been frequently interpreted as placing limitations on laws and legal proceedings, in order for judges instead of legislators to guarantee fundamental fairness, justice, and liberty.
Constitution	A constitution is a system that establishes the rules and principles that govern an organization or political entity.
Welfare	Welfare is financial assistance paid by taxpayers to groups of people who are unable to support themselves, and determined to be able to function more effectively with financial assistance.
Referendum	A referendum is a direct vote in which an entire electorate is asked to either accept or reject a particular proposal. This may be the adoption of a new constitution, a constitutional amendment, a law, the recall of an elected official or simply a specific government policy. The referendum is a form of direct democracy.
Local government	Local government are administrative offices that are smaller than a state or province. The term is used to contrast with offices at nation-state level, which are referred to as the central government, national government, or (where appropriate) federal government.
Equal protection clause	The Equal Protection Clause, part of the Fourteenth Amendment to the United States Constitution, provides that "no state shall deny to any person within its jurisdiction the equal protection of the laws." The Equal Protection Clause can be seen as an attempt to secure the promise of the United States' professed commitment to the proposition that "all men are created equal" by empowering the judiciary to enforce that principle against the states.
First Amendment	The First Amendment to the United States Constitution is a part of the United States Bill of Rights. It prohibits the federal legislature from making laws that establish religion or prohibit free exercise of religion, laws that infringe the freedom of
Court of Appeal	Court of Appeal is the title of a court which has the power to consider or hear an appeal. A court of appeal is also a superior court.
Human rights	Human rights refers to universal rights of people regardless of jurisdiction or other factors, such as ethnicity, age, nationality, sexual orientation or religion.
Criminal law	Criminal law is the body of statutory and common law that deals with crime and the legal punishment of criminal offenses. It is law prohibiting conduct that disrupts social order or challenge's the authority of the state, and consequently deals with matters of significant public concern. In contrast with civil law, actions are pursued by the state rather than private citizens.

Go to Cram101.com for the Practice Tests for this Chapter.

Chapter 16. Are Laws Criminalizing Homosexual Conduct Unconstitutional?

Chapter 16. Are Laws Criminalizing Homosexual Conduct Unconstitutional?

Civil liberties	Civil liberties is the name given to freedoms that completely protect the individual from government. Civil liberties set limits for government so that it can not abuse its power and interfere with the lives of its citizens.
Commonwealth	Commonwealth originally meant a state governed for the common good as opposed to an authoritarian state governed for the benefit of a given class of owners. Today the term is more general and means a political community.
Concurring opinion	In law, a concurring opinion is a written opinion by some of the judges of a court which agrees with the majority of the court but might arrive there in a different manner. In a concurring opinion, the author agrees with the decision of the court but normally states reasons different from those in the court opinion as the basis for his or her decision. When no absolute majority of the court can agree on the basis for deciding the case, the decision of the court may be contained in a number of concurring opinions, and the concurring opinion joined by the greatest number of jurists is referred to as the plurality opinion.
Mandate	In international law, a mandate is a binding obligation issued from an inter-governmental organization like the United Nations to a country which is bound to follow the instructions of the organization.
Autonomy	Autonomy means freedom from external authority. In politics, autonomy refers to self-governance.
Legislation	Legislation is law which has been promulgated (or "enacted") by a legislature or other governing body. The term may refer to a single law, or the collective body of enacted law, while "statute" is also used to refer to a single law. Before an item of legislation becomes law it may be known as a bill, which is typically also known as "legislation" while it remains under active consideration.
Misdemeanor	A misdemeanor in many common law legal systems, is a "lesser" criminal act. Misdemeanors are generally punished less severely than felonies; but theoretically more so than administrative infractions (also known as regulatory offenses).
Jurisdiction	In law, jurisdiction is the practical authority granted to a formally constituted legal body or to a political leader to deal with and make pronouncements on legal matters and, by implication, to administer justice within a defined area of responsibility.
Doctrine	Doctrine is a body of axioms fundamental to the exercise of a nation's foreign policy. Hence, doctrine, in this sense, has come to suggest a broad consistency that holds true across a spectrum of acts and actions.
Stare decisis	Stare decisis (Latin: [sta¢°re de¢° ki¢°si¢°s], Anglicisation: [sta¢° i də sa s s], "to stand by things decided") is a Latin legal term, used in common law to express the notion that prior court decisions must be recognized as precedents, according to case law. More fully, the legal term is "stare decisis et non quieta movere" meaning "stand by decisions and do not move that which is quiet" (the phrase "quieta non movere" is itself a famous maxim akin to "let sleeping dogs lie").
Case law	Case law the body of judge-made law and legal decisions that interprets prior case law, statutes and other legal authority -- including doctrinal writings by legal scholars such as the Corpus Juris Secundum, Halsbury's Laws of England or the doctrinal writings found in the Recueil Dalloz and law commissions such as the American Law Institute.
Strict scrutiny	Strict scrutiny is the penultimate standard of judicial review used by United States courts reviewing federal law (the most exacting standard, "super strict scrutiny," is used to review prior restraints outside of the Near v. Minnesota exception). Along with the lower standards of rational basis review and intermediate scrutiny, strict scrutiny is part of a hierarchy of standards courts employ to weigh an asserted government interest against a constitutional

Go to Cram101.com for the Practice Tests for this Chapter.

Chapter 16. Are Laws Criminalizing Homosexual Conduct Unconstitutional?

Chapter 16. Are Laws Criminalizing Homosexual Conduct Unconstitutional?

	right or policy that conflicts with the manner in which the interest is being pursued.
Legitimacy	Legitimacy in political science, is the popular acceptance of a governing regime or law as an authority. Where as authority refers to a specific position in an established government, the term legitimacy is used when describing a system of government itself —where "government may be generalized to mean the wider "sphere of influence."
Rule of law	The rule of law is the principle that governmental authority is legitimately exercised only in accordance with written, publicly disclosed laws adopted and enforced in accordance with established procedure.
Plurality	A plurality, relative majority or simple majority is the largest share of something, which may or may not be considered a majority, i.e. it is the largest group/category, but is not necessarily a majority (more than half). In the U.S., simple majority has another meaning. The plurality voting system, also known as "First past the post", elects the candidate who is the stated first choice of the plurality of voters.
Regime	A regime is the set of rules, both formal and informal that regulate the operation of government and its interactions with the economy and society.
Common law	In common law legal systems, judges have the authority and duty to decide what the law is when there is no other authoritative statement of the law. Once an appellate court has decided what the law is, that precedent tends to bind future decisions of the same appellate court, and binds all lower courts reviewed by that appellate court, when the facts of the case are similar, until there is another authoritative statement of the law.
Bill of Rights	A bill of rights is a list or summary of which is considered important and essential by a group of people. The purpose of these bills is to protect those rights against infringement by other people and the government.
Civil rights	Civil rights are the protections and privileges of personal power given to all citizens by law. Civil rights are distinguished from "human rights" or "natural rights", also called "our God-given rights". They are rights that are bestowed by nations on those within their territorial boundaries, while natural or human rights are rights that many scholars claim should belong to all people.
Constitutional law	Constitutional law is the study of foundational or basic laws of nation states and other political organizations. Constitutions are the framework for government and may limit or define the authority and procedure of political bodies to execute new laws and regulations.
Litigation	A lawsuit, also known as litigation, is a criminal or civil action brought before a court in which the party commencing the action, the plaintiff, seeks a legal remedy. Often, one or more defendants are required to answer the plaintiff's complaint.

Chapter 16. Are Laws Criminalizing Homosexual Conduct Unconstitutional?

Chapter 17. Damages in Cases of Student-on-Student Sexual Harassment?

Majority opinion	In law, a majority opinion is a judicial opinion agreed to by a majority of the members of a court. A majority opinion sets forth the decision of the court and an explanation of the rationale behind the court's decision.
Supreme Court	The supreme court functions as a court of last resort whose rulings cannot be challenged, in some countries, provinces and states. However, in some jurisdictions other phrases are used to describe the highest courts. There are also some jurisdictions where the supreme court is not the highest court.
Dissenting opinion	A dissenting opinion is an opinion of one or more judges expressing disagreement with the majority opinion. A dissenting opinion cannot create binding precedent because the holding in the opinion is not the holding of the court in the case.
Citizenship	Citizenship is membership in a political community and carries with it rights to political participation; a person having such membership is a citizen. It is largely coterminous with nationality, although it is possible to have a nationality without being a citizen ; it is also possible to have political rights without being a national of a state.
Court of Appeal	Court of Appeal is the title of a court which has the power to consider or hear an appeal. A court of appeal is also a superior court.
Legislation	Legislation is law which has been promulgated (or "enacted") by a legislature or other governing body. The term may refer to a single law, or the collective body of enacted law, while "statute" is also used to refer to a single law. Before an item of legislation becomes law it may be known as a bill, which is typically also known as "legislation" while it remains under active consideration.
Third party	In any two-party system of politics, a third party is a party other than the two dominant ones. While technically the term is limited to the third largest party, it is often used as (innumerate) shorthand to describe any smaller party.
Common law	In common law legal systems, judges have the authority and duty to decide what the law is when there is no other authoritative statement of the law. Once an appellate court has decided what the law is, that precedent tends to bind future decisions of the same appellate court, and binds all lower courts reviewed by that appellate court, when the facts of the case are similar, until there is another authoritative statement of the law.
Plaintiff	A plaintiff is the party who initiates a lawsuit before a court. By doing so, the plaintiff seeks a legal remedy, and if successful, the court will issue judgment in favor of the plaintiff and make the appropriate court order .
Federalism	Federalism is a political philosophy in which a group of members are bound together with a governing representative head. The term federalism is also used to describe a system of government in which sovereignty is constitutionally divided between a central governing authority and constituent political units.
Constitution	A constitution is a system that establishes the rules and principles that govern an organization or political entity.
Litigation	A lawsuit, also known as litigation, is a criminal or civil action brought before a court in which the party commencing the action, the plaintiff, seeks a legal remedy. Often, one or more defendants are required to answer the plaintiff's complaint.
Due process	In United States law, adopted from English Law, due process is the principle that the government must normally respect all of a person's legal rights instead of just some or most of those legal rights when the government deprives a person of life, liberty, or property. Due process has also been frequently interpreted as placing limitations on laws and legal proceedings, in order for judges instead of legislators to guarantee fundamental fairness, justice, and liberty.

Chapter 17. Damages in Cases of Student-on-Student Sexual Harassment?

Chapter 17. Damages in Cases of Student-on-Student Sexual Harassment?

First Amendment	The First Amendment to the United States Constitution is a part of the United States Bill of Rights. It prohibits the federal legislature from making laws that establish religion or prohibit free exercise of religion, laws that infringe the freedom of
Mandate	In international law, a mandate is a binding obligation issued from an inter-governmental organization like the United Nations to a country which is bound to follow the instructions of the organization.
Logistics	**Logistics** is the art and science of managing and controlling the flow of goods, energy, information and other resources like products, services, and people, from the source of production to the marketplace. It is difficult to accomplish any marketing or manufacturing without logistical support.
Autonomy	Autonomy means freedom from external authority. In politics, autonomy refers to self-governance.

Chapter 17. Damages in Cases of Student-on-Student Sexual Harassment?

Chapter 18. Extraordinary Care to Attend Regular Classes in Public Schools

Majority opinion	In law, a majority opinion is a judicial opinion agreed to by a majority of the members of a court. A majority opinion sets forth the decision of the court and an explanation of the rationale behind the court's decision.
Supreme Court	The supreme court functions as a court of last resort whose rulings cannot be challenged, in some countries, provinces and states. However, in some jurisdictions other phrases are used to describe the highest courts. There are also some jurisdictions where the supreme court is not the highest court.
Dissenting opinion	A dissenting opinion is an opinion of one or more judges expressing disagreement with the majority opinion. A dissenting opinion cannot create binding precedent because the holding in the opinion is not the holding of the court in the case.
Legislation	Legislation is law which has been promulgated (or "enacted") by a legislature or other governing body. The term may refer to a single law, or the collective body of enacted law, while "statute" is also used to refer to a single law. Before an item of legislation becomes law it may be known as a bill, which is typically also known as "legislation" while it remains under active consideration.
Administrative law	Administrative law is the body of law that arises from the activities of administrative agencies of government. Government agency action can include rulemaking, adjudication, or the enforcement of a specific regulatory agenda.
Administrative law judge	An administrative law judge in the United States is an official who presides at an administrative trial-type hearing to resolve a dispute between a government agency and someone affected by a decision of that agency. It is the initial trier of fact and decision maker.
Court of Appeal	Court of Appeal is the title of a court which has the power to consider or hear an appeal. A court of appeal is also a superior court.
Income tax	An income tax is a tax levied on the financial income of persons, corporations, or other legal entities. Various income tax systems exist, with varying degrees of tax incidence. Income taxation can be progressive, proportional, or regressive. When the tax is levied on the income of companies, it is often called a corporate tax, corporate income tax, or profit
Legitimacy	Legitimacy in political science, is the popular acceptance of a governing regime or law as an authority. Where as authority refers to a specific position in an established government, the term legitimacy is used when describing a system of government itself —where "government may be generalized to mean the wider "sphere of influence."
Federalism	Federalism is a political philosophy in which a group of members are bound together with a governing representative head. The term federalism is also used to describe a system of government in which sovereignty is constitutionally divided between a central governing authority and constituent political units.
Rehnquist	Rehnquist was an American lawyer, jurist, and a political figure, who served as an Associate Justice on the Supreme Court of the United States and later as the Chief Justice of the United States. Rehnquist favored a federalism under which the states meaningfully exercised governmental power.
Mandate	In international law, a mandate is a binding obligation issued from an inter-governmental organization like the United Nations to a country which is bound to follow the instructions of the organization.

Go to **Cram101.com** for the Practice Tests for this Chapter.

Chapter 18. Extraordinary Care to Attend Regular Classes in Public Schools

Chapter 19. Race-Conscious Programs in Public University Admissions Policies

Dissenting opinion	A dissenting opinion is an opinion of one or more judges expressing disagreement with the majority opinion. A dissenting opinion cannot create binding precedent because the holding in the opinion is not the holding of the court in the case.
Supreme Court	The supreme court functions as a court of last resort whose rulings cannot be challenged, in some countries, provinces and states. However, in some jurisdictions other phrases are used to describe the highest courts. There are also some jurisdictions where the supreme court is not the highest court.
Majority opinion	In law, a majority opinion is a judicial opinion agreed to by a majority of the members of a court. A majority opinion sets forth the decision of the court and an explanation of the rationale behind the court's decision.
Equal protection clause	The Equal Protection Clause, part of the Fourteenth Amendment to the United States Constitution, provides that "no state shall deny to any person within its jurisdiction the equal protection of the laws." The Equal Protection Clause can be seen as an attempt to secure the promise of the United States' professed commitment to the proposition that "all men are created equal" by empowering the judiciary to enforce that principle against the states.
Affirmative action	Affirmative action refers to concrete steps that are taken both to increase the representation of underrepresented and arguably underprivileged minorities and to redress the effects of past discrimination. The idea of this policy is that making sure to put discriminated minorities in positions of prestige and authority will eliminate discrimination both because it will counteract the prejudice of those who give out jobs, admit to universities, etc. and because it will demonstrate that members of those groups can accomplish great things if given the opportunity.
Litigation	A lawsuit, also known as litigation, is a criminal or civil action brought before a court in which the party commencing the action, the plaintiff, seeks a legal remedy. Often, one or more defendants are required to answer the plaintiff's complaint.
Class action	Class action is a procedural device used in litigation to determine the rights of and remedies, if any, for large numbers of people whose cases involve common questions of law and fact.
Court of Appeal	Court of Appeal is the title of a court which has the power to consider or hear an appeal. A court of appeal is also a superior court.
Constitution	A constitution is a system that establishes the rules and principles that govern an organization or political entity.
Status quo	Status quo is a Latin termpresent, current, existing state of affairs. To maintain the status quo is to keep the things the way they presently are. The related phrase status quo ante, means "the state of things as it was before."
Constituent	A constituent is someone who can or does appoint or elect another as their agent or representative.
Stare decisis	Stare decisis (Latin: [sta¢°re de¢° ki¢°si¢°s], Anglicisation: [sta¢° i də sa s s], "to stand by things decided") is a Latin legal term, used in common law to express the notion that prior court decisions must be recognized as precedents, according to case law. More fully, the legal term is "stare decisis et non quieta movere" meaning "stand by decisions and do not move that which is quiet" (the phrase "quieta non movere" is itself a famous maxim akin to "let sleeping dogs lie").
Strict scrutiny	Strict scrutiny is the penultimate standard of judicial review used by United States courts reviewing federal law (the most exacting standard, "super strict scrutiny," is used to review prior restraints outside of the Near v. Minnesota exception). Along with the lower standards

Chapter 19. Race-Conscious Programs in Public University Admissions Policies

Chapter 19. Race-Conscious Programs in Public University Admissions Policies

	of rational basis review and intermediate scrutiny, strict scrutiny is part of a hierarchy of standards courts employ to weigh an asserted government interest against a constitutional right or policy that conflicts with the manner in which the interest is being pursued.
First Amendment	The First Amendment to the United States Constitution is a part of the United States Bill of Rights. It prohibits the federal legislature from making laws that establish religion or prohibit free exercise of religion, laws that infringe the freedom of
Meritocracy	Meritocracy is a system of government or other organization based on demonstrated ability and talent rather than by wealth, family connections, class privilege, cronyism, popularity or other historical determinants of social position and political power.
Regime	A regime is the set of rules, both formal and informal that regulate the operation of government and its interactions with the economy and society.
Amicus curiae	Amicus curiae, is a legal Latin phrase, literally translated as "friend of the court", that refers to someone, not a party to a case, who volunteers to offer information on a point of law or some other aspect of the case to assist the court in deciding a matter before it. The information may be a legal opinion in the form of a brief - testimony that has not been solicited by any of the parties - or a learned treatise on a matter that bears on the case. The decision whether to admit the information lies with the discretion of the court.
Desegregation	Desegregation is the process of ending racial segregation, most commonly used in reference to the United States. Desegregation was long a focus of the American Civil Rights Movement, both before and after the United States Supreme Court's decision in Brown v. Board of Education, particularly desegregation of the school systems and the military, as was the closely related but somewhat more ambitious goal of racial integration.
Declaration of Independence	The United States Declaration of Independence was an act of the Second Continental Congress, adopted on July 4, 1776, which declared that the Thirteen Colonies were independent of the Kingdom of Florida.
Courts of appeals	Courts of Appeals or Court of Appeal is the title of a court which has the power to consider or hear an appeal. A court of appeal is also a superior court
Jurisdiction	In law, jurisdiction is the practical authority granted to a formally constituted legal body or to a political leader to deal with and make pronouncements on legal matters and, by implication, to administer justice within a defined area of responsibility.
Doctrine	Doctrine is a body of axioms fundamental to the exercise of a nation's foreign policy. Hence, doctrine, in this sense, has come to suggest a broad consistency that holds true across a spectrum of acts and actions.
Plurality	A plurality, relative majority or simple majority is the largest share of something, which may or may not be considered a majority, i.e. it is the largest group/category, but is not necessarily a majority (more than half). In the U.S., simple majority has another meaning. The plurality voting system, also known as "First past the post", elects the candidate who is the stated first choice of the plurality of voters.
Autonomy	Autonomy means freedom from external authority. In politics, autonomy refers to self-governance.
National security	National security refers to the requirement to maintain the survival of the nation-state through the use of economic, military and political power and the exercise of diplomacy.
Citizenship	Citizenship is membership in a political community and carries with it rights to political participation; a person having such membership is a citizen. It is largely coterminous with nationality, although it is possible to have a nationality without being a citizen ; it is also possible to have political rights without being a national of a state.

Go to **Cram101.com** for the Practice Tests for this Chapter.

Chapter 19. Race-Conscious Programs in Public University Admissions Policies

Chapter 19. Race-Conscious Programs in Public University Admissions Policies

Legitimacy	Legitimacy in political science, is the popular acceptance of a governing regime or law as an authority. Where as authority refers to a specific position in an established government, the term legitimacy is used when describing a system of government itself —where "government may be generalized to mean the wider "sphere of influence."
Mandate	In international law, a mandate is a binding obligation issued from an inter-governmental organization like the United Nations to a country which is bound to follow the instructions of the organization.
Civil rights	Civil rights are the protections and privileges of personal power given to all citizens by law. Civil rights are distinguished from "human rights" or "natural rights", also called "our God-given rights". They are rights that are bestowed by nations on those within their territorial boundaries, while natural or human rights are rights that many scholars claim should belong to all people.
Public interest	The public interest refers to the "common well-being" or "general welfare." The public interest is central to policy debates, politics, democracy and the nature of government itself. While nearly everyone claims that aiding the common well-being or general welfare is positive, there is little, if any, consensus on what exactly constitutes the public interest.
Representation	In politics, representation describes how residents of a country are empowered in the government. Representation usually refers to representative democracies, where elected representatives speak for their constituents in the legislature. Generally, only citizens are granted representation in the government in the form of voting rights, however some democracies have extended this right further.
Electronic media	Electronic media are media that utilize electronics or electromechanical energy for the end user, which are most often created electronically, but don't require electronics to be accessed by the end user in the printed form.
World Wide Web	World Wide Web is a system of interlinked, hypertext documents accessed via the Internet. With a Web browser, a user views Web pages that may contain text, images, and other multimedia and navigates between them using hyperlinks.
Case law	Case law the body of judge-made law and legal decisions that interprets prior case law, statutes and other legal authority -- including doctrinal writings by legal scholars such as the Corpus Juris Secundum, Halsbury's Laws of England or the doctrinal writings found in the Recueil Dalloz and law commissions such as the American Law Institute.

Printed in the United States
112349LV00003B/155-158/A